The *Promise*
of
Heschel

The Promise of Theology
Martin E. Marty, General Editor

The Promise
of
Heschel

by
FRANKLIN SHERMAN

J. B. LIPPINCOTT COMPANY
Philadelphia and New York

To Joan

Foreword

One winter evening I bumped into Abraham Joshua Heschel in a hotel in Jerusalem. That sentence makes me vulnerable to the charge of name-dropping, and I plead guilty. What better name to drop, and what better way to introduce this man than personally? He can't be dealt with abstractly, as a propounder of doctrines or formulator of theories. Rabbi Heschel gave me three of those potent cigars mentioned by Professor Sherman on the pages following. The promise of a pleasant evening was ahead.

Within an hour we were deeply immersed in the question of Israel, a topic close to Heschel's soul. Then came the subject of death; he wanted to try out some ideas he was to present the next week to a medical conference in Italy. A third topic came up when he observed that the twentieth-century theological revival had not been matched by similar creativity in the realm of spiritual writing. Could I think of any theological thinkers who have made contributions to that field? The answer was simple: "You have!"

That hour in Israel and my report on it serve as typical approaches to Heschel's mode, and the mode is part of the message, in his case. His theology is born of personal experience, molded into narrative as an interpretation of a people's history, tinged with a mystical and soul-full sense, never afraid to take on the big questions.

Professor Sherman develops these Heschelian themes in

the following pages; never extravagant or reckless in his praise, he does find it difficult to come up with anything profoundly negative or critical. Professor Heschel, for all his prophetic power, comes into one's world as a dispeller of negation, one who brings hope and affirmation out of others.

As editor I have to keep a critical eye on each of the manuscripts in this series; let me confess that while others may have introduced me to more complicated systems of thought, more intricate theories, more carefully developed approaches to theology, none was so moving as this one. Heschel's work is directed not only to the mind but also to the heart and to the will.

"The promise of Heschel," so evident in this book and in that evening in Jerusalem, was confirmed for me by an invitation I do not intend to forget to share some year in the *Seder* at his home. Readers of this book will no doubt feel some envy at the invitation and some surprise that I have not yet taken him up on it. But there are other aspects of Heschel's promise and each of us can find his own.

MARTIN E. MARTY
The University of Chicago

Contents

I

A Prophetic Voice in Our Midst

As the decade of the 1960's moved onward from its hopeful beginnings through the ordeal of assassinations, urban crises, and protracted war to the opening of yet another new frontier in outer space, a disquieting voice was heard increasingly throughout America. The voice was that of Rabbi Abraham Joshua Heschel. On college and university campuses, at Christian seminaries as well as Jewish rabbinical assemblies, at colloquies on race relations and in the corridors of power, he spoke on the sensitive and difficult problems of the day in the best tradition of the Western conscience and of its biblical roots.

Even in his physical appearance conjuring up the image of what an Amos or an Isaiah must have looked like—stocky, full-bearded, speaking softly but with passionate intensity—it is small wonder that many viewed him as a latter-day Hebrew prophet. Heschel would reject the title, since, according to Jewish teaching, prophecy ceased in biblical times; yet in the adjectival sense, his was surely a "prophetic" voice. He himself provided the best description of what it would mean to stand in this tradition.

"The prophet," he wrote, "is a man who feels fiercely. God has thrust a burden upon his soul, and he is bowed and stunned at man's fierce greed."

> Frightful is the agony of man; no human voice can convey its full terror. Prophecy is the voice that God has lent to the silent agony, a voice to the plundered poor, to the profaned riches of the world. . . . God is raging in the prophet's words.[1]*

* Superior figures refer to the Notes at the end of the text.

Note some of the presuppositions of this brief statement, all of which we shall find echoing throughout Heschel's works: (1) *the reality of God,* not as a distant, unmoved mover but as a vivid presence; (2) *the predicament of man,* who debases and despoils God's creation, including human society; (3) *the possibility of reciprocity between God and man,* of shared concern and collaborative action toward renewal. All of these themes deserve further exploration.

But first, let us look into some of the specifics of Heschel's indictment of contemporary culture, and in the process learn something more of the man himself. About what does he "feel fiercely"?

Best known to the general public, undoubtedly, is Heschel's concern and action on the two issues which themselves have been pivotal during these years: those of race and peace. On the former issue, many will remember the picture of him striding alongside Dr. Martin Luther King, Jr., in the famous protest march at Selma, Alabama, in the spring of 1965. Visibly Jewish, he helped to symbolize, along with the priests and nuns in their distinctive garb, the tri-faith unity for the cause of freedom and racial justice. Not as well known was Heschel's prominent role at the National Conference on Religion and Race in Chicago in early 1963, which sparked churchmen's participation in the great "march on Washington" later that year. Heschel delivered the keynote address.

"One hundred years ago the emancipation was proclaimed," he reminded the delegates. "It is time for the white man to strive for *self-emancipation,* to set himself free of bigotry." The greatest sin, he declared, is that of indifference. "That equality is a good thing, a fine goal, may be generally accepted. What is lacking is a sense of the *monstrosity of inequality.*" He called for a "total mobilization of heart, intelligence, and wealth for the purpose of love and justice."[2]

In still more recent years, Professor Heschel has been featured in the mass media as a leader in the protest against American policy in Southeast Asia, especially in his capacity as national co-chairman of the organization called Clergy and Laity Concerned about Vietnam. Perhaps by the time these words appear in print the immediate questions of political and military strategy for extricating the United States from that involvement will have been resolved. But the underlying moral and historical questions will remain: What does this bitter experience teach us about ourselves? About the limits of technological power? About the relation between means and ends? About the nature of the revolutionary trends in the non-Western world?

It was at this deeper level that Abraham Heschel's protest was directed. To withdraw from Vietnam would no doubt mean losing face, he admitted (he understood the dilemmas of the policy-makers), but to remain there would mean something worse: losing our souls. He saw the continuation and escalation of the war as another instance of that moral callousness, that insensitivity to the sufferings of others combined with an overweening confidence in the rightness of one's own position, that underlay America's racial problem. And so he called—long before this became a theme of political campaigns—for national repentance, for a return to conscience and an enlargement of the moral imagination, for a dedication to peace rather than victory. In particular he appealed to those of religious faith. "To speak about God and remain silent on Vietnam," he warned, "is blasphemous."[3]

A similar effort to penetrate to the deeper levels of a problem characterized Heschel's other public utterances during this period. In 1960, at the White House Conference on Children and Youth, he pushed the question back to the issue of the quality of life in our whole society. "The problem of our youth is not youth," he declared.

> The problem is the spirit of our age: denial of transcendence, the vapidity of values, emptiness in the heart, the decreased sensitivity to the imponderable quality of the spirit, the collapse of communication between the realm of tradition and the inner world of the individual. . . .

The problem will not be solved by implanting in the youth a sense of belonging. Belonging to a society that fails in offering opportunities to satisfy authentic human needs will not soothe the sense of frustration and rebellion.[4]

The ensuing decade of unprecedented restiveness among American youth and students may well be thought to have confirmed the accuracy of this prophetic "prediction."

Professor Heschel spoke similarly at the White House Conference on Aging held the following year. What does the widespread fear of growing old tell us about our culture? It tells us that we suffer from what Heschel calls "the fear of time." Space we can master, and the things of space (whether ordinary goods or sophisticated technical achievements) become our servants. But we shrink inwardly from the problem of structuring time, and we are crushed by the irreversibility of its onward movement. "Time is the only aspect of existence which is completely beyond man's control." Yet it is precisely here, Heschel asserts, that God confronts us: in the occasions, the decisions, and the events of time. It is here where the issue between meaning and meaninglessness is joined. Fulfillment can be found only by going out to meet God, who is the source of meaning, where he seeks to meet us—in the continuum of time. This means, on society's part, planning for significant involvement rather than isolation of the elderly. And it means, on the part of the individual, a frank acceptance of the aging process, and a lifelong preparation for the opportunities which leisure brings for the enrichment of one's inner being. In truth, as Heschel observes, the years of old age may be regarded as "formative years, rich in possibilities to unlearn the follies of a lifetime."[5]

These are but glimpses of the activities and utterances of a man who, as we have said, has been heard increasingly in recent years across the land. In many ways, his role as an interpreter of the religious tradition and as a spokesman on the leading issues of the day is comparable to that played somewhat earlier by Reinhold Niebuhr (who is Heschel's close personal friend). And, as in the case of Niebuhr, many who have been attracted by Heschel's insights on secular issues have learned somewhat to their surprise that underlying these outjuttings of relevance is a vast corpus of theological reflection and research. It is time that we, too, inquire concerning these further dimensions of the man and of his work.

Abraham Joshua Heschel, like another great theologian of our time, Paul Tillich, is a gift from Europe to America. And as in the case of Tillich, his coming to this country was the direct result of the repressive measures introduced by the Nazi regime in Germany. Heschel, however, is Polish in origin. Born in 1907 in Warsaw, he received his early education entirely within the world of the intensive Jewish piety of Eastern European Judaism. The son and grandson of Hasidic rabbis, and the more remote descendant of a line of scholars and religious leaders stretching back to the sixteenth century, he was clearly destined for a life of study. In late adolescence, however, he faced the crucial choice of whether his studies should continue to be only within the world of Jewish learning—Bible, Talmud, and the mystical tradition—or whether he should enter the world of modern, secular scholarship as represented by the great German universities. He chose the latter, and in 1927 enrolled in the University of Berlin. There, in the faculty of philosophy in which he studied, the school of phenomenology was at its height—a viewpoint which was to have its influence on his later work. But while appreciatively absorbing the riches of the modern intellectual tradition, he remembered with equal appreciation the world of fervent faith and piety from which he had come; and he resolved to try to hold these two worlds together. He would neither forsake his faith in order to adjust to the modern world, nor retreat from the world in order to preserve his faith. Rather, he would allow each element to criticize as well as to fructify the other: this is the program we can see

Heschel following to the present time.

It was logical, therefore, that he should enroll also at the *Hochschule für die Wissenschaft des Judentums* (Academy for Jewish Studies) in Berlin. There, in 1932-1933, he assumed his first teaching post as an instructor in Talmud. The Ph.D. degree was awarded him by the University of Berlin in 1933. His dissertation dealt with the subject of prophecy, *die Prophetie,* from the phenomenological, theological, and literary perspectives, as well as in the light of comparative religion. Published in German in 1935, this study underlay especially the latter half of Heschel's massive volume, *The Prophets,* published in English in 1962.[6]

Now he launched into the field of adult education, and in 1937 had the honor to be chosen as successor to Martin Buber at the *Jüdisches Lehrhaus* in Frankfurt. But the scope for such activities was narrowing as the Nazis introduced ever stricter anti-Semitic measures. In 1938 came the order expelling all Jews of Polish citizenship from Germany. Heschel returned to Warsaw, where he taught briefly at a rabbinical seminary, but in the summer of 1939, less than two months before the German invasion of Poland that marked the outbreak of the Second World War, he departed for London.

Thus Abraham Heschel narrowly escaped the fate that was to befall his fellow Jews on the "dark continent" that Europe became under Nazi rule. The story of what happened to the Jews of Warsaw has been told in John Hersey's novel *The Wall*—their forced resettlement, all 500,000 of them, within the confines of a walled ghetto; their harassment, intimidation, deprivation, degradation, starvation, and eventual annihilation despite a heroic uprising. In Europe as a whole, three out of every four Jews perished. The dimensions of such a tragedy are inconceivable, and needless to say, Abraham Heschel has not forgotten it. Listen to the opening words of the lecture he gave some twenty-five years later upon assuming the Harry

Emerson Fosdick Visiting Professorship at Union Theological Seminary:

> I speak as a member of a congregation whose founder was Abraham, and the name of my rabbi is Moses.
>
> I speak as a person who was able to leave Warsaw, the city in which I was born, just six weeks before the disaster began. My destination was New York, it would have been Auschwitz or Treblinka. I am a brand plucked from the fire, in which my people was burned to death. I am a brand plucked from the fire of an altar of Satan on which millions of human lives were exterminated to evil's greater glory, and on which so much else was consumed: the divine image of so many human beings, many people's faith in the God of justice and compassion, and much of the secret and power of attachment to the Bible bred and cherished in the hearts of men for nearly two thousand years.[7]

Is it any wonder that Heschel's voice was both eloquent and insistent when in subsequent years he pleaded for aid for Jews suffering persecution in the Soviet Union, as well as for the State of Israel—refuge of those few who were saved from the Holocaust—when it, too, was threatened with annihilation by encircling foes?[8]

London proved to be only a way station on Heschel's pilgrimage. In 1940, he proceeded to the United States, where he had received a call to join the faculty of Hebrew Union College in Cincinnati, Ohio. The chair which he filled was that of Jewish Philosophy and Rabbinics. In America, Heschel found himself once again in the midst of conflict between the old and the new, between tradition and modernity, as expressed especially in the familiar distinction between Orthodox, Conservative, and Reform Judaism. It is significant that Heschel remained only five years at Cincinnati, the outpost of the Reform position, which has gone furthest in adjusting both Jewish thought and practice to modern assumptions and conditions. In 1945, he accepted a call to the chair of Jewish Ethics and Mysticism at the Jewish Theological Seminary of America. Strategically located across the street from Union Theo-

[17]

logical Seminary and adjacent to the campus of Columbia University, Jewish Theological Seminary is the center of the Conservative movement. It has served as Heschel's base of operations for the past quarter century.

Professor Heschel became a naturalized citizen of the United States in 1945. In the following year, he was married to Sylvia Straus, a gifted pianist from Cleveland, Ohio, whom he had met while teaching at Cincinnati. The Heschels' home, in which both Jewish and Gentile guests are made to feel welcome, is a pleasant apartment on Riverside Drive just a few blocks from the Seminary. Their daughter, Hannah Susannah, is now a student at Trinity College, preparing for a career in medicine.

Noteworthy aspects of Abraham Heschel's career, in addition to the public appearances referred to at the beginning of this chapter, have been his terms of service as visiting professor in departments of religious thought at secular state universities (Minnesota, 1960, and Iowa, 1961); his West Memorial Lectures at Stanford University in 1963; and his year as visiting professor at Union Theological Seminary, 1965-1966. The chief milestones in his career during these years, however, have been the publication of his major books, which now number almost a dozen. First to appear, significantly, was the slender, eloquent volume in which Heschel sought to memorialize the now-vanished faith and culture of his homeland. *The Earth is the Lord's: The Inner World of the Jew in East Europe* was published in 1950 in a handsome edition, illustrated with a most remarkable set of wood engravings by Ilya Schor. The book is not, perhaps, in the strictest sense a work of scholarship, carefully analyzing and categorizing its subject matter. Rather, it is a primary document, which itself represents the spirit and the style of life that it depicts. Only enough historical background and sociological detail is introduced to enable the reader to view in context that which is of chief concern: the way in which the profound religious faith of these communities expressed itself in a life of worship, study of Scripture and tradition, and a unique combination of self-discipline and *joie de vivre.* We shall have occasion to refer further to this memorable exposition of the meaning of Jewishness.

In 1951 there appeared Heschel's study entitled *The Sabbath: Its Meaning for Modern Man.* Note both the title and the subtitle in this case. The Sabbath, a venerable Jewish observance, is to be interpreted in terms of "its meaning for modern man"—a typical Heschel enterprise, linking an ancient heritage with the modern situation. In many ways, this is a companion volume to *The Earth Is the Lord's*; they are of roughly the same size and nature and are illustrated by the same artist. Not surprisingly, then, when the two works were reissued a decade later they were published within the covers of one volume.

Meanwhile, there had appeared also in 1951 the book which probably first brought Abraham J. Heschel to the attention of a broader reading public, beyond the circle of those concerned with Judaism as such. Again, the basic affirmation of the volume was evident in its title—*Man Is Not Alone: A Philosophy of Religion.* In later years, when the so-called "death-of-God theology" was in its heyday, Heschel was to refer to his position as a "Living God theology."[9] He had already thrown down that gauntlet in this early book. His target there, however, was not so much that strange breed of untheological theologians but, rather, the secular man on the street, whose coming of age might well be celebrated, but in whose life there might yet be an aching void where God used to be. If a man had become so callous that he no longer felt the ache, then his last state was worse than his first. Much of Heschel's analysis and prescription in this book is devoted to such a man.

Man Is Not Alone had been announced as the first part of a two-volume work. Four years later appeared the sequel, entitled *God in Search of Man: A Philosophy of Judaism.* In a very rough sense, the first volume deals with

God in general (and religion in general), while the second deals with God as specifically known in the biblical revelation (and with Judaism as a specific response). The two overlap, however, the first including also some specifically Jewish themes, while the second recapitulates much of the apologetic groundwork. This element of repetition has proved annoying to some readers. No doubt it was partly with them in mind that one of Heschel's younger colleagues (and a former pupil), Fritz A. Rothschild, at this point prepared an anthology of Heschel's writings, designed to embody in compact form the essence of his thought. Published in 1959 under the title *Between God and Man: An Interpretation of Judaism, from the Writings of Abraham J. Heschel,* it included selections from the works surveyed above, from the manuscript of his book on the prophets, and from other published and unpublished essays and articles.

Then, in 1962, came publication of Heschel's massive work *The Prophets,* to which we have already referred. The first part of the book consists chiefly of an interpretive survey and commentary on the writings of particular prophets: Amos, Hosea, Isaiah, Micah, Jeremiah, Habakkuk, and Second Isaiah. The remaining chapters, which incorporate most of Heschel's earlier book in German on the subject, deal with such cross-sectional themes as the prophetic view of history, of justice and judgment, and of the divine-human relationship as a whole, as well as with diverse theories of prophetic inspiration. It is here that Heschel develops the contrast between the biblical "God of pathos" and the Hellenic concept of the immovability of the divine, as well as between what he calls the "religion of sympathy" corresponding to the former, and the "religion of apathy" corresponding to the latter.

Professor Heschel's next book, *Who Is Man?* has also already been alluded to. Modest in size, but concise and even aphoristic in its language, it is presented as a prolegomenon to a longer study of the question of man. The direction of Heschel's thrust is clear: against all forms of reductionism, he seeks to awaken an awareness of the fullest dimensions of "being human," which includes openness to the transcendent, acknowledgment of the fragility as well as the nobility of human life, and a sense of indebtedness both to God and to man. Human living is not simply "being-in-the-world" or "being thrown into the world," he concludes, in contrast to the secular existentialists; it is "being-challenged-in-the-world."[10]

In addition to the foregoing, two other volumes have been published containing collections of Heschel's essays, papers, and journal articles (though they include only a small proportion of his total output). The volume *Man's Quest for God: Studies in Prayer and Symbolism* appeared in 1954, and is focused on the subject indicated. Then, in 1966, there appeared *The Insecurity of Freedom: Essays on Human Existence.* These are grouped into three parts, the first presenting statements on contemporary problems, including the lectures on race, youth, etc., that we cited above; the second containing essays on more strictly theological questions and on interfaith dialogue; and the third dealing with explicitly Jewish topics, including liturgy, religious education, the plight of the Jews in the Soviet Union, and the role of the State of Israel.

Abraham Heschel had always had a deep attachment to the State of Israel, and the crisis of the "six-day war" of 1967 challenged him into giving theological expression to his views. The murderous threats leveled at Israel by its Arab foes on every side, the arming of these nations by a major-power bloc, the withdrawal of the United Nations peace-keeping force, and the seeming unconcern of the United States raised once again the specter of annihilation of this very people which had suffered so unspeakably in Europe. Heschel writes that he felt that his own existence was at stake. Yet many Christians and even some Jews in the United States apparently could not understand why one should be so agitated about the matter. It was to speak to this situation that Heschel wrote his book *Israel: An Echo of Eternity,* which was published in early 1969.

The book is a paean of love for the land, for its people, for its heritage. In many passages, it is more nearly poetry than prose. Yet the book also contains a carefully reasoned apologia for the Jews' reclamation of their homeland, and a discussion of the significance of this event for Christian and Jewish theology. This volume, in fact, contains the most extended discussion of the question of Messianic expectation to be found anywhere in Heschel. The pivotal question is whether and to what extent the return might be regarded as a fulfillment of such expectation.

The books surveyed above are Heschel's major works in English (for a complete list of his essays and journal articles, see the Rothschild anthology). To round out the picture of Heschel's scholarship, we should mention at least two works written in other languages: his biography of the great medieval Jewish thinker Maimonides, published in Germany in 1935; and his massive work being written and published in Hebrew, *Torah min ha-shamayim* (literally, "Torah from Heaven"), a study of types of rabbinic theology. Two volumes of this latter study have been published, in 1962 and 1965, and a third is expected; reviewers have hailed it as Heschel's *magnum opus.*

This, then, is the thinker in whose promise we are interested. In the case of a living theologian, "promise" can refer to that which we anticipate he may yet produce; and certainly there is every reason to expect further significant works from Heschel's pen. But it can also refer, as in the case of a theologian of a past decade or century, to unappropriated riches in that which he has already done. There is enough of the latter in Heschel's thought to occupy us fully in this study. Even within the Jewish community itself, though his work has been received most cordially, there is ample scope for its further influence, calling Judaism to an ever deeper, more theological self-understanding. As for Christians, we have hardly begun to explore the significance of having in our midst, in modern America, such a spokesman for the very tradition of the prophets and the psalmists in which our own faith is rooted. Christianity claims to have gone beyond Judaism, and in terms of its acceptance of Jesus as Messiah, it clearly has. Yet Christianity may have much to learn—perhaps not about the final affirmations but about the foundational elements of its faith—from those who speak out of the context of a continued covenant with the God of Abraham, Isaac, and Jacob.

Finally, there is promise in the thought of Abraham Joshua Heschel for those who may not be committed Jews or Christians, but who value the humanity of man and are concerned with the plight of contemporary culture. They will learn, however, that Heschel insists that the question of man cannot be solved apart from the question of God, who is the locus of meaning as well as mystery in man's life. It is with this question that we begin our more detailed exposition of Heschel's thought.

II

God as Presence and Pathos

Early in the present century, a prominent American philosopher wrote a book entitled *The Meaning of God in Human Experience.* Though it may not have satisfied all the specifics of traditional belief, William Ernest Hocking's work had considerable influence as an apologia for theism. Fifty years later, theologians themselves were writing books with such titles as *The Death of God.* What had transpired in the meantime? Does the outcry "God is dead" inform us of something that has happened to God, or of something that has happened to man—to his culture, his quality of life, his capacity for faith?

Abraham J. Heschel is one who suspects that the latter is the case. "Some of us," he writes, "are like patients in the state of final agony—who scream in delirium: the doctor is dead, the doctor is dead."[1]

Heschel thus agrees with those who state that the flurry of recent talk about the death of God really betokens man's own sickness unto death. Yet he does not rest content with this assertion, as if it adequately solved the problem. He realizes that a closer diagnosis of the malady is called for, and furthermore, that the real aim is to enable man to recover from this sickness, i.e., to reawaken to the reality of God. To this end, it is necessary to analyze what is really meant by "God," and what there might be about the inherited idea of God that could lead to the reports of his demise.

But how can we mortal and muddled men adequately describe or define the God who—if he be real—so far outstrips the power of our words? Precisely this problem troubles Heschel; but he feels that to take it seriously is the beginning of wisdom in theology. A God who is fully graspable would not be the God of biblical faith. "My thoughts are not your thoughts, neither are your ways my ways, says the Lord." The prerequisite for knowledge of God, says Heschel in his basic work *Man Is Not Alone,* is "the sense of the ineffable." Though it comes to be almost a technical term in Heschel, a dictionary definition[2] of "ineffable" is remarkably suggestive of the way in which he uses it:

1. Too overpowering to be expressed in words: *ineffable* joy.
2. Too lofty or sacred to be uttered: the *ineffable* name of Jehovah. 3. Indescribable; indefinable.

Elsewhere Heschel speaks of this dimension as the dimension of "mystery," or of "the sublime," or as the "holy dimension," By whatever name, it stands for that which transcends our capacity to understand or to express, and yet which, paradoxically, is known to us—known by direct experience. Heschel illustrates with reference to man's attitude toward nature. Three aspects of nature, he points out, command our attention: its power, its loveliness, and its grandeur. Its power we exploit; its loveliness we enjoy; but before its grandeur, we stand in awe. This indeed is the proper attitude when faced with the ineffable. Heschel also calls it "radical amazement." It is akin, no doubt, to that sense of wonder in which Plato says all philosophy begins.

The ineffable, or the realm of mystery, should not simply be equated with the unknown. It lies not only at the edge of knowledge but also at the root of that which may seem to be well known. The sense of the ineffable, states Heschel, involves the recognition that "what is intelligible to our minds is but a thin surface of the profoundly undisclosed."

> The ineffable inhabits the magnificent and the common, the grandiose and the tiny facts of reality alike. Some people sense this quality at distant intervals in extraordinary events; others sense it in the ordinary events, in every fold, in every nook; day after day, hour after hour.... Slight and simple as things may be—a piece of paper, a morsel of bread, a word, a sigh—they hide and guard a never-ending secret: A glimpse of God? Kinship with the spirit of being? An eternal flash of a will?[3]

Heschel's use here of the question-form, rather than direct assertion, is significant. The ineffable does not provide us with a proof of God's existence; it only hints at him.

The world, says Heschel, is like an open house in which the presence of the owner is so well concealed that we mistake his discretion for nonexistence. God, in other words, is revealed in his creation; yet he is revealed in the form of hiddenness. It requires a special sensitivity, therefore, to become aware of him. The capacity for such sensitivity, Heschel asserts, is deep-rooted in every man. It is given with our very nature. Yet it may become terribly clouded over by the distractions of daily life, especially in an acquisitive and affluent society. Religion, then, at its best, becomes a profounder form of "sensitivity training," to use a current phrase. It is a therapy for callousness.

Heschel is speaking here, as readers will recognize, of what Baron von Hügel has called "the mystical element in religion," or what Tillich calls the "mystical *a priori*" on which all theologizing rests. There must be an element of immediacy, of direct experience of the divine, which precedes our efforts to conceptualize it. Heschel indeed acknowledges his indebtedness to the mystical tradition, and has devoted much effort to interpreting its role in Jewish thought (his chair, it will be remembered, is that of "Jewish Ethics and Mysticism"). Contrary to the notion of Judaism as a pedestrian, merely secular or ethical religion, he points out that both the biblical tradition and later Jewish piety are well acquainted with the thought of inwardness, of religious ecstasy, of transrational experience involving union or communion with the divine. The Psalms are a font of such an attitude; the Song of Solomon, or Song of Songs, was thus interpreted; medieval Judaism was suffused with mysticism; and in modern times it had an upsurge in the Hasidic movement. All these are representative of those who, in Heschel's vivid phrase describing the aspirations of the mystic, "want to taste the whole wheat of spirit before it is ground by the millstones of reason."[4]

A further word will be in order here about the Hasidic movement, to which we have already alluded more than once, and which forms the most immediate religious background for Heschel's thought, including his doctrine of God. The word *hasidim* (plural of *hasid*) means literally "the pious ones." In ancient Judaism, it was applied to those fervent believers at the time of the Maccabees (second century B.C.) who proved most uncompromising in the face of the temptations of Hellenism. Later it was applied also to certain medieval mystics. But the word is used more commonly to denote the movement resulting from the work of the great eighteenth-century Jewish rabbi and reformer, Israel ben Eliezer, known as the Baal Shem Tov ("Master of the Good Name"). The Besht, as he is also known from the initial letters of his appellation, was a mystic with a difference. He stressed God's presence to the common man and in the common life, and the dominant motif of his preaching was not ascetic mortification but joy in God's creation. In this latter, to be sure, he was only accentuating the major trend in Jewish mysticism through the ages, which, as Heschel points out, has never been alien to the finite. Judaism has found the infinite not apart from but "in, with, and under" the finite, if we may use the Lutheran phrase in this connection.

In the Baal Shem's time, this message was received with special gratitude, coming as it did in the midst of a period of suffering and disappointment. There had been a wave of anti-Semitic persecutions, on the one hand, and on the other, the sad collapse of the Messianic expectations that had recently flared up (Shabbati Zevi, a mid-seventeenth-century figure widely hailed as the Messiah, ended his days as a convert to Islam). The prevailing orthodoxy offered little spiritual sustenance at such a time, and the Hasidic movement came like a river of refreshment to a dry and thirsty land. In this respect as well as others, Hasidism bore a remarkable resemblance to the movement within Protestantism with which it was roughly contemporaneous—namely, Pietism. Both stressed life rather than doctrine; personal faith rather than mere assent to the tradition; and direct study of the Scriptures by all believers. Like Pietism, the Hasidic movement gained numerous followers, who organized themselves into conventicles that coexisted in some tension with the surrounding religious community. Again, like Pietism, when the threat of modernism arose (for Judaism, in the form of *Haskalah*, the Jewish Enlightenment), Hasidism moved into a defensive alliance with the Orthodoxy against which it had protested. Not only compromise with modern culture in behavior or belief, but even the study of secular learning was taboo for the Hasidim. It was with this tradition that Abraham Heschel had to break, as we have seen, when he went to study at the University of Berlin. And it is this same intellectual monasticism on the part of the Hasidim that has prevented Heschel from relating himself to the surviving Hasidic communities in the United States, such as the Hungarian-American group in the Williamsburg area of Brooklyn, New York. [5]

Nevertheless, there is something even in this defensive attitude of Hasidism that is akin to Heschel's stance. On the one hand, he wants to vivify the tradition, to internalize it, and to simplify it; in this respect he appears as a reformer over against orthodoxy, just as had the Besht. On the other hand, he is equally concerned to preserve the true substance of the tradition from the disintergrating acids of modernity. It is the existence of continuing communities of those who share these concerns that gives Heschel as theologian or philosopher of religion the material with which to work.

For it is as true of the whole range of religion and religious belief as it is of the doctrine of God: first must come the reality, then the analysis. Note how Heschel defines, in *Man Is Not Alone,* the task of the philosophy of religion: it is the analysis of "that which is immediately given with the pious man."[6] Here the influence of Heschel's studies in phenomenology reveals itself. The task, in the first instance, is not to defend or to explain but to understand the phenomena; not to prove something, but to penetrate into the nature of that which confronts us. Heschel, to be sure, does not rest content with this *epoche,* or suspended judgment; he goes on to argue for the realty and relevance of that which religion speaks of. Yet first things must come first.

(What, then, do we learn from the Hasidic movement or ✓ from the Jewish mystical tradition in general about the nature and reality of God as experienced by the believer? At this point we may hazard two generalizations, which are framed in our own words rather than Heschel's. First, that *God is a dimensional reality;* i.e., that he is encountered not so much as a discrete object which may or may not be there, but as a dimension—a quality or context in and around all other objects—of which we may or may not be aware. This proposition has a corollary: that the "knowledge of God" means not the gaining of new information, but the learning of a new way of seeing. A further corollary would be that "the death of God" refers to our loss of this capacity.)

Certainly this does not dispose of the "death-of-God" problem, and furthermore, if this were all that were to be said, one might well charge this view with being essentially pantheistic rather than a reflection of the faith of Abraham, Isaac, and Jacob. There *is* more to be said, but at the foundational level such an assertion can serve as testimony to the divinity of the divine. Perhaps it is inherent in a faith that takes seriously both God's omnipresence and his hiddenness that it will be mistaken for pantheism, on the one hand, and for atheism, on the other.

Heschel deals with this theme by expounding the biblical category of the "glory of God," which he describes as "the effulgence of God's presence." The whole earth is full of his glory, as Isaiah perceived in his great vision of the Holy One. Yet this presence is not wholly evident, so that it must also be said that the glory of the Lord "shall be" revealed (Isaiah 40:5).

This brings us to our second generalization from the Jewish mystical tradition, which is that *God and his creation are not antithetical.* They are distinct, yes; but not inherently opposed to one another. Rather, the creation as such is the theater of God's glory. That of which this cannot be said is to be charged not to God but to man and to his sin. We alluded to this theme above in speaking of the interpenetration—or, to speak more Hebraically, the mutual embrace—of finite and infinite. There is a corollary here, too, which pertains to the death-of-God debate: namely, that it is not necessary to deny God in order to exalt man. As Dietrich Bonhoeffer and the later Barth have insisted, "God is *for* man." Jewish mysticism, says Heschel, "aims at the elevation and expansion of existence."[7]

Such a position, however, need not involve a reduction of God to the human plane or an uncritical affirmation of all things human. God, who is truly present, also is transcendent, both ontologically and ethically. He is transcendent ontologically by virtue of the fact that his *being* is not exhausted by his *presence* in the world. God, says Heschel, lies on a tangent to the curve of human experience. It is to protect God's transcendence that Heschel rejects Tillich's phrase "the ground of being". He prefers to speak of God as "being in and beyond all beings." Even more concretely, he speaks of God as "One Who brings others into being," and "One Who cares for other beings."[8]

Further, God is transcendent ethically, by virtue of his holiness, which stands in tension with all that detracts from the ennoblement of his creation. Jewish mysticism and the Jewish tradition as a whole have a profound sense of the turbulent forces at work beneath the seemingly placid surface of human life, and of the destructive effects of man's *yetzer ha-ra* (the "evil impulse," drive, or imagination; see Genesis 6:5). Man's task is to collaborate with God in the redemption both of his own life and of the world from such evil.

With these considerations, however, we are moving to the realm in which Heschel's thought is more distinctively informed by the prophetic than by the mystical tradition. These two elements or types of religion have often been contrasted with one another. Mysticism has been seen as more otherworldly, prophetic religion as more thisworldly; mysticism as more impersonal in its conception of God, prophetism as more personal; mysticism as concentrating more on self-fulfillment, prophetism on servanthood (as in Nygren's contrast of *eros* and *agape*). Heschel himself draws this contrast very strongly in his book *The Prophets,* where he is concerned to reject the theory that prophetic inspiration could be explained, reductively, as a form of mystic ecstasy—i.e., as a merely subjective experience rather than a real vision or audition of the divine. Yet in his other works, as we have seen, one of his dominant concerns is to appropriate the Jewish mystical tradition; and in his study of the prophets themselves, he shows how important to them was the element of immediacy in their relationship to God, which is the essence of the mystical. Furthermore, they were not strangers to supernormal states of consciousness.

We prefer to conclude, therefore, that the mystical and the prophetic are to be viewed as complementary rather than contradictory types of religiousness. The prophets, in their own way, were mystics, and the this-worldly mysticism of later Judaism (and, in part, of Christianity) shows the influence of the prophetic faith. Abraham Heschel himself, after all, has written both a book with the title *Man's Quest for God,* dealing primarily with prayer (a special concern of the mystic), and another entitled *God In Search of Man,* which tries to present the essence of biblical (i.e.,prophetic) faith. The two standpoints are combined in a key statement in the latter book: "It is within man's power to seek Him; it is not within his power to find Him." [9] Both human and divine initiatives are required.

It is of interest to note that Heschel's work on the prophets, picking up his earlier academic interest and resulting finally in his massive book *The Prophets,* published in 1962, corresponded in time with his own emergence as a spokesman on social issues of the day. This is no coincidence, by his own acknowledgment. Study of the prophets drove him to social concern. Nor, perhaps, is it a coincidence that the same development took place in the life of the great Maimonides, whose biography Heschel wrote. Expert as a philosopher, theologian, natural scientist, mathematician, and jurist, Maimonides devoted the last years of his life to service as a physician.

> This is Maimonides' metamorphosis: From metaphysics to medicine, from contemplation to practice, from speculation to the imitation of God. . . . Preoccupation with the concrete man and the effort to aid him in his suffering is now the form of religious devotion.[10]

"Preoccupation with the concrete man," especially the suffering man—this is characteristic also of the prophets. But their great insight is that *God himself* is thus concerned with the concrete man. We have referred above to Heschel's description of the prophet as a man who "feels fiercely," who is deeply moved with compassion at human need or with indignation at man's greed. The prophets proclaim, however, that it is God who, in the first instance, is thus moved. They only serve as his spokesmen in reporting—and embodying—his reactions. Prophetic religion, in Heschel's phrase, is a "religion of sympathy" in the sense of a "feeling with" God's own feelings.

The word "feelings" could easily be misinterpreted in a superficial or sentimental way. For this reason, it is good that Heschel employs a technical term at this point: he speaks of "the divine pathos." Prophetic thought, in turn, is referred to as a "theology of pathos."[11] Let us take note of some elements of this idea as Heschel sets it forth in his examination of the writings of the prophets.

The prophet Amos proclaims God's judgment on his people, his wrath upon those who "sell the needy for a pair of shoes, and trample the head of the poor into the dust of the earth." Yet he pleads with God to "repent," to turn aside from his wrath. Amos does not conceive of God as a mechanical principle of justice; it is possible that his mercy may yet prevail.

Hosea accentuates this note of God's compassion, indeed his passion, for his people. "God is conceived, not as the self-detached Ruler, but as the sensitive Consort to Whom deception comes and Who nevertheless goes on pleading for loyalty. . . ."[12] Hosea's emotional identification with this attitude of God, his sympathy with the divine pathos, is shown in the parallelism of his own marital experience. Of interest in this connection is Hosea's frequent use of the term *daath elohim*, usually rendered "the knowledge of God." As has often been pointed out, the verb "to know" in biblical Hebrew can also refer to sexual union. Heschel interprets it an implying a total interpersonal relationship, with emphasis on the emotional nexus. *Daath elohim* thus connotes an intimacy with God, a sympathy and sensitivity for what concerns him, a sharing of experience.

The prophet Isaiah, extending Amos' vision of Yahweh's judging not only Israel but also the surrounding peoples, proclaims God's sovereignty over the whole of history. In the name of the God who interferes with the plans of men, the prophet himself interferes in Israel's politics. He articulates God's sorrow over Israel's apostasy, his impatience with her folly, his determination to bring about—in his own good time—a purgation that shall be both judgment and renewal.

Jeremiah, above all, exhibits the suffering that must come to the prophetic soul that lives in sympathy with God. For God himself is afflicted in the afflictions of his people. God's anguish, rage, compassion all surge through the prophet's bones. Jeremiah is a good example of the prophet's double identification, with both God and man. Standing before God, he pleads for the people; standing before the people, he pleads for God and for obedience to his holy will. Jeremiah's hope of a "new covenant" involves an extension of such sympathy with God to all: "for they shall all know me, from the least of them to the greatest, says the Lord" (Jeremiah 31:34).

The prophet Habakkuk, dealt with briefly by Heschel, articulates the divine-human relationship in terms of trust or faith. Even in the midst of destruction, he is able to "rejoice in the Lord." Finally, the Second Isaiah (chaps. 40-66) arises to speak in majestic tones. The climax of his message, extending that of Jeremiah, is his proclamation of *God's involvement in the sufferings of men*—and of the obedient one's involvement in God's involvement. The suffering servant of the Lord (who for Heschel is Israel) shares the grief of God as well as men, and serves as the vehicle of the divine compassion.

All these things are well known to any reader of the Bible, yet they have seldom been adequately reckoned with in formal theology. This Heschel sees as the unfortunate result of the supervening of the Hellenic upon the Hebraic tradition, even in Jewish circles. A less anthropomorphic God was called for; the God who changes in response to human situations was rejected. Thus Maimonides, for example, denied all "passibility" (capacity for feeling or for suffering) in God, as did the Christian theologians, who had to resort to a complex Christology and doctrine of the Trinity in order to hold together the notion of the Incarnation and the reality of the sufferings of Christ. (Yet the Bible speaks plainly of God's pain and anguish at the plight of man, as well as the further range of emotions we have reviewed.

Strictly speaking, this is not "anthropomorphism," but "anthropopathy," as Heschel points out; not man's form, but his feelings, are in question. Still, the analogy to the human remains. But in what other way shall we speak of God? If man is the crown of creation, to speak of God in analogy to anything else would be to reduce his grandeur. As Heschel puts it, the "anaesthetization" of God would be just as much a pitfall as his undue "humanization." Surely the Greek notion of a-pathy (*apatheia,* complete freedom from emotions), whether as a description of God or as an ideal for man, is not superior to the biblical notion of God's pathos and man's sym-pathy. We are reminded of Dietrich Bonhoeffer's affirmation: "Only the suffering God can help."[13]

Actually, as Heschel points out, the biblical view is not that God is to be thought of in analogy to man, but that man is to be thought of in analogy to God, and is to be brought concretely—i.e., ethically and emotionally—into such an analogy. As Heschel remarks:

> The idea of the divine pathos combining absolute selflessness with supreme concern for the poor and the exploited can hardly be regarded as the attribution of human characteristics. Where is the man who is endowed with such characteristics? Nowhere in the Bible is man charactized as merciful, gracious, slow to anger, abundant in love and truth, keeping love to the thousandth generation. . . .
> God's unconditional concern for justice is not an anthropomorphism. Rather man's concern for justice is a theomorphism.[14]

Abraham Heschel's great service in expounding this notion of the divine pathos, and other aspects of the meaning of a genuinely "Living" God, may be said to be twofold. First, he has provided a good deal of raw material for contemporary theology. The reader will perhaps have noticed some striking resemblances between Heschel's views and those of contemporary theologians and philosophers of religion such as Charles Hartshorne who are trying to rethink the doctrine of God in terms of Whiteheadian metaphysics—i.e., in terms of process, rather than changelessness, as the basic category. Likewise, there is an affinity with Kierkegaard and with the later existentialists who take human dynamics as the clue to ontology. A thorough analysis of the relation of his thought to these other schemes is beyond the scope of our discussion here, however. It is not made easier by the somewhat elusive as well as allusive character of Heschel's thought, in comparison to that of more systematic (and perhaps less imaginative) theologians. What can surely be said is that Heschel has explored and expounded the *biblical* materials far more thoroughly than any of these other thinkers. In this respect, especially, he provides raw material for further work in theology.

Heschel's other great service is to the common man, who suffers a credibility gap between his daily experience and the idea of God. Far from anthropopathy being an obstacle, it may well be that for contemporary man the idea of a God who is involved and concerned with the details of human affairs is much more believable than is the concept of an unmoved mover or a distant cosmic principle. Human life is so fascinating, so tragic, so exhilarating, that a God who ignored or despised it could hardly be credited as a still-living God.

When all this has been said, however, it is still true that God's being transcends the power of our conceiving, even if we do find relatively more adequate categories. Just as the Lord says, in the words of the prophet, "My thoughts are not your thoughts," so also, Heschel acknowleages, might he say, "My pathos is not your pathos." The prophets do not claim to know God's essence; they speak only of his presence, of the forms of his relatedness to the world.

Perhaps it is this fear of reducing God to the limits of our categories that causes Heschel, despite all his emphasis on the anthropopathic element in the divine, to reject the proposition that God is "a person." To move from the adjectival or descriptive phrase (God as "personal") to the substantive or definitional one (God as "a person") is a step he declines to take. He does this, however, not because to say that God is a person would be to say too much about him, but because it would be to say too little. God transcends the distinction between the personal and the impersonal, just as he trancends the distinction between the now and the then, the here and the there.

Heschel reports with approval an ancient rabbinic discussion about the question of God's "place" in the world. Actually, the rabbis conclude, God does not *have* a place in the world; rather, he *is* the place *of* the world. Thus the term *Maqom* ("place") can serve in the Talmud as a synonym for the Ineffable Name. As Heschel himself puts it, "God is the circle moving around humanity."[15] Only when the majesty of God's transcendence over *all* our categories is appreciated can we appreciate in turn the prophets' paradoxical assertion that this Transcendent One wills to be Immanent for man, that he cherishes, pursues, rebukes, and redeems his creatures.

III

The Meaning of Being Human

Abraham Heschel's major work on the subject of the present chapter bears the unusual title *Who is Man?* The pronoun "who" is chosen, even in the face of the biblical precedent (Psalm 8: "What is man that thou art mindful of him?"), in order at the very outset to guard against what Heschel sees as the grave danger of depersonalization in contemporary culture. Man today must learn to understand himself as a uniquely centered self, a "who," rather than a "what"—a merely physical, biological, sexual, statistical, economic, or political entity. All these latter, though they convey partial truth, lead too easily to what Heschel calls "metonymical misunderstandings"—taking a part for the whole.

Beyond the special sciences, therefore, which deal with particular aspects of human nature (biology, psychology, sociology, etc.), there is need for philosophical or theological reflection on man's nature as a whole. *Who is Man?* is an exercise in such reflection. This brief volume, which combines with Heschel's usual eloquence a remarkable lucidity, might well serve the reader as an introduction to his thought. Before reviewing its contents here, we want to examine again some aspects of his earlier writing, looking especially at the implications for a concept of *man* of the understanding of *God* that Heschel has articulated.

That there should be a close connection between these two factors is inevitable, in Heschel's or any other scheme of thought. Man's life, it might be said, presents us with a text to be interpreted; we seek its meaning. But a text can be properly interpreted only in its *context.* We are driven to ask, therefore: What is the reality surrounding man? What is its character, its quality or structure? Depending on how man reads the context, he will give a different exegesis of the text of his own life. If, for example, he views the universe merely as a cold machine, an automated mechanism, he will be tempted to view his own life in the same way. If he sees nothing in nature but the struggle for existence, he will have little incentive to interpret human existence any differently. But if he acknowledges that at the root of reality there is a living God, then he is challenged to understand himself in terms of the fullest livingness, and to shape his life in accordance with the nature of this God. Perhaps this is part of what is meant by the biblical concept of man's being made in God's image. The same would be true no matter what sort of god one conceived or worshiped. As Augustine asserted, "A man becomes what he loves."

We have spoken about God, in the first place, in terms of "the ineffable." The ineffable, to be sure, is not identical with God. Rather, God is a Presence that meets us in the dimension of the ineffable. But if we are not sensitive to this dimension, we shall hardly meet that Presence. Recall, then, the aspects of the ineffable as catalogued in the definition that we cited (see p. 25): the overpowering; the lofty; the indefinable. To such things, what is the appropriate response? In each case, humility—whether in view of our weakness in the face of that which has the power to shatter us; or of our sordidness in the face of the holy; or of the limited capacity of our minds to "say what we see." If a sense of the ineffable is essential to any awareness of the full context of our lives and hence to proper self-definition, then we may say, as a first principle, that *true humanity begins in humility.*

Several terms are suggested by Heschel for this basic

attitude which the sense of the ineffable evokes. He calls it "reverence." This would be reverence in a generalized sense, somewhat like Albert Schweitzer's "reverence for life," since the ineffable is a dimension even of ordinary objects and experiences. He also calls it "appreciation," reminding us of Bernard Meland's phrase "appreciative awareness."[1] The opposite, in either case, is the attitude of exploitation or manipulation—the assumption that the world is there for my enhancement and deserves to be brought under my control. This contrast provides us with a set of categories very similar to Martin Buber's "I–Thou" and "I–It" relations. One can take either an appreciative or manipulative attitude toward the world of nature, toward other people, toward God, and even toward oneself.

This last theme, that of the attitude toward oneself, is handled with especial sensitivity by Heschel. The normal assumption would be that, however many things I do not know, I surely understand quite well that which is closest to me, namely, myself. But Heschel points out that even here we have the paradox of "the unknown within the known." Despite all the efforts of modern science and philosophy, the essence of selfhood remains undefinable—in the strictest sense, ineffable.

> The self cannot be described in the terms of the mind, for all our symbols are too poor to render it. The self is more than we dream of; it stands, as it were, with its back to the mind. Indeed, to the mind even the mind itself is more enigmatic than a star.[2]

The ineffable, then, exists not only outside of me; it intersects my own being. The mystery of selfhood corresponds with the mystery of God. Such an awareness puts me on guard against all reductionist explanations of human nature, and against too small an estimate of my own destiny.

But this is not all there is to be said, for we move on from the general, mystic sense of the ineffable to the specifics of the prophetic faith. Here we have to do with revelation—with something added to that which is available and analyzable at the depths of every man's existence. "In the prophets the ineffable became a voice.... Out of stillness of endless ages came compassion and guidance."[3] The prophets tell us of the divine initiative and the divine pathos. What does this add to our concept of man?

We can say two things on the basis of Heschel's discussion: to be human means *to be known,* and it means *to be needed.*

Both of these are reversals of our normal way of thinking. Consider the first. We usually think of man in his active capacity as a knower, busy in pursuing knowledge, storing and utilizing it. But here we speak in the passive voice of man's being known. Known by whom? By no one, obviously, if the universe is empty of any living presence except man's; the conception then would be meaningless. But if at the heart of things there is a living Presence, a divine Subject ... then the totality of my life is open to that Knowing One. Then it is the case, not that God is a thought in my mind, but that I am a thought in the mind of God.

> To the philosopher God is an *object,* to men at prayer He is the *subject.* Their aim is not to possess Him as a concept of knowledge, to be informed about Him, as if He were a fact among facts. What they crave for is to be wholly possessed by Him, to be an object of His knowledge and to sense it. The task is not to know the unknown but to be penetrated with it; *not to know* but *to be known* to Him, to expose ourselves to Him rather than Him to us; not to judge and to assert but to listen and to be judged by Him.[4]

It is on the basis of this line of thinking that Heschel can declare, in one of his best-known aphorisms, "The Bible is not man's theology but God's anthropology."[5]

To be human is to be known by God: Heschel's thought here stands in a venerable tradition. The psalmist declares, "O Lord, thou hast searched me and known me!" The apostle Paul states of the day of eschatological fulfillment: "Then shall I know even as also I am known" (I Corinthians 13:12, AV). And one of the great prayers of confession in the Christian tradition begins, "O Lord, unto whom all hearts are open, all desires known. . . ." All these, including Heschel's formulation, may be regarded as more dynamic ways of stating what is intended by the classic doctrine of God's "omniscience," with the accent on what this means for the man who is the object of God's knowing. (Similarly, what we said about God as a "dimensional" reality could be seen as a restatement of his "omnipresence.")

Second, we said that to be human is to be needed. Again, this is a reversal of our customary viewpoint. We know that to be human means to *need* many things: food, shelter, affection, etc. Some of these represent a biological or psychological minimum that is prerequisite to the maintenance of life itself. But beyond these, there is a tremendous range of culturally relative needs—"learned" needs, as it were, which may be expanded *ad infinitum.* Heschel is most critical of modern advertising for attempting to persuade us that true humanity is to be found somewhere—always a little further—along the range of the fulfillment of such needs. The prophets, in contrast, teach us that man's greatness is to be found in the fact that he *is needed* for something that transcends him. The Eternal God himself needs man for the effecting of his purposes in the world and true fulfillment is to be found in the free acceptance of these purposes and the realignment of one's life so as to accord with them.

"It is a most significant fact," Heschel notes, "that man is not sufficient to himself, that life is not meaningful to him unless it is serving an end beyond itself, unless it is of value to someone else." A common cause of neurosis, he points out, is the sense of futility that accompanies the feeling of being useless. "Happiness," he concludes—before the making of such formulations became a fad—"may be defined as the *certainty of being needed.*"[6]

The same point is made in a more extended discussion of the "meaning of meaning," where Heschel inveighs against a purely subjective interpretation of the term.[7] Meaning is not simply something I bestow upon reality. It is something that I read off from reality. This assumption, says Heschel, lies at the basis of all scientific study of the regularities of nature. But the same is true of our human life. Before ever I can raise the question of the meaning of my life, it must be the case that I exist; and if I ask why I exist at all, I am asking about an objective meaning. This quest is answered by the prophetic faith in God as Subject. Before ever I can seek or posit meanings, I *am* a meaning in the mind of God. "Existence is a compliance," says Heschel.[8] He might well have proposed a formula in Cartesian style: "I am meant, therefore I am."

In all these ways as well as others (for he has many versions of the same basic point), Abraham Heschel is trying to teach us once again what it would really mean to acknowledge ourselves as *creatures,* and to let our self-understanding be governed by this acknowledgment. To admit one's creaturehood means really to take seriously that "man is not alone"; that I am known before I know; that my self is not self-posited but has been willed into existence by another. Life lived in the acknowledgment of creaturehood means at the same time exaltation—for I am related to the purposes of the transcendent God—and limitation. It means, in short, life on the human scale.

If Heschel thus has an equivalent to what Christian theology calls the doctrine of Creation, does he have an equivalent to what it calls the doctrine of the Fall? The answer here is twofold. He does not have any specific, substantive term corresponding to "the Fall." But *verbally* and *adjectivally* he points to those sorts of attitudes and actions, and their consequences, whose ubiquity in human history provides the data that this concept was originally designed to interpret. Here again, Heschel is being typically Hebraic; his thought is dynamic and descriptive rather than static or systematizing in character.

Given the fact that this is his mode of thought, however, we can say that there is in Heschel an indictment of the actual state of human affairs that equals in severity anything pronounced by a Christian theologian. This is only to be expected from one who stands in the heritage of the psalmist who declares:

> The Lord looks down from heaven upon the children of men,
>   to see if there are any that act wisely,
>   that seek after God.
>
> They have all gone astray, they are all alike corrupt;
>   there is none that does good,
>   no, not one.
>
> (Psalm 14:2-3)

And of the prophet who proclaims:

> There is no truth, no love, and no knowledge of God in the land;
> Swearing and lying, killing and stealing, and committing adultery,
> They break all bonds, and blood touches blood.[9]
>
> (Hosea 4:1-2)

In fact it is a special mark of a prophet, according to Heschel, that he has what to ordinary men seems an exaggerated sensitivity to evil. His voice is too shrill, his diagnosis overly severe.

"To us," writes Heschel, "a single act of injustice—cheating in business, exploitation of the poor—is slight; to the prophets, a disaster. To us injustice is injurious to the welfare of the people; to the prophets it is a deathblow to existence."[10] It is because he thinks theologically and theopathically that the prophet speaks in such decisive terms. One of the key functions of revelation is to induce in us a comparable sensitivity, to overcome our "callousness to catastrophe."

(One of the most poignant of Abraham Heschel's utterances is the address which he delivered to a meeting of

Quakers at Frankfurt, Germany, in March, 1938, just a few months before he was forced to leave the country. First published in an expanded version in 1943, it was printed with some further modifications as the final chapter of *Man's Quest for God* in 1954. These are its opening sentences; it is not hard to envision the circumstances that called them forth:

> Emblazoned over the gates of the world in which we live is the escutcheon of the demons. The mark of Cain in the face of man has come to overshadow the likeness of God. There has never been so much guilt and distress, agony, and terror. At no time has the earth been so soaked with blood. Fellowmen turned out to be evil ghosts, monstrous and weird.

Heschel declines to take the easy way out, to put the blame on a few evil men. He speaks confessionally: "We have failed to fight *for* right, *for* justice, *for* goodness; as a result we must fight *against* wrong, *against* injustice, *against* evil." The "we" even includes previous generations:

> Our world seems not unlike a pit of snakes. We did not sink into the pit in 1939, or even in 1933. We had descended into it generations ago, and the snakes have sent their venom into the bloodstream of humanity, gradually paralyzing us, numbing nerve after nerve, dulling our minds, darkening our vision. Good and evil, that once were as real as day and night, have become a blurred mist. In our every-day life we worshipped force, despised compassion, and obeyed no law but our unappeasable appetite. The vision of the sacred has all but died in the soul of man.[11]

Heschel left Germany and came to the United States in order to escape such terror. Some thirty years later, after having become a fully loyal member of the American community, he finds it necessary to speak out against similar forms of inhumanity within America itself (race prejudice, neglect of the old and the poor, unthinking conformism) or perpetrated by this country's forces elsewhere in the world (the Vietnam war). Abraham Heschel himself, we should note, has not made a direct equation between the situation here and that in Nazi Germany, as have some critics. Heschel's respect for historical accuracy and for this country's heritage is too great for that. But we, who cannot help but notice how his career spans these two situations, may legitimately make the connection, and take it as a call to national repentance.

The possibility of repentance: this is the factor that prevents the dark view of contemporary history that we find in Heschel from resulting in utter hopelessness. This and one other factor: his tenacious faith in God's own promise of a day when the results of man's rapacity will be wiped away. Both of these are aspects of the prophetic heritage. What saved the prophets from despair, asserts Heschel, was "their messianic vision and their idea of man's capacity for repentance." On these grounds, they held that history was still open to renewal.

> History is not a blind alley, and guilt is not an abyss. There is always a way that leads out of guilt: repentance or turning to God. The prophet is a person who living in dismay has the power to transcend his dismay. Over all the darkness of experience hovers the vision of a different day.[12]

This theme of hope—hope in the face of disaster—plays a major role in Heschel's exposition of prophetic faith in his book *The Prophets*. Behind the prophet's severity, as behind the severity of God, is compassion. The prophet desires to offer not false consolation, to be sure, but the assurance that upon repentance and return a new beginning will yet be possible. Nearly every prophet, though he begins with a message of doom, ends with a message of hope (Heschel does not accept the scholarly conjecture which would eliminate these passages from the pre-exilic prophets). It is by reason of this openness that the main task of the prophet cannot be to *predict* but, rather, to *persuade*. The outcome of history does depend on man's response.

Heschel further discusses the theme of hope in his book

Israel: An Echo of Eternity. The capacity to hope is what sustained the vision of a return to the Holy Land that was finally fulfilled in our own time. "Perhaps the most characteristic quality of Jewish existence," Heschel observes, "is *bittahon* ('hope')." It is integral to Jewish existence "to be faithful to the future, to keep alive the beginning by nursing the vision of the end."[13] Hope, he says, is the creative articulation of faith. A biblical equivalent for it is the term "waiting," as in the psalmist's cry, "I wait for the Lord, my soul waits, and in his word I hope" (Psalm 130:5). Waiting is not a passive attitude. It can be combined with strenuous effort. It does imply, however, that "the success of all human efforts toward redemption [remains] contingent and indecisive without God's action."[14]

The question of meaning in history is seen by Heschel as closely related to this question of hope. Sounding like one of the recent Christian spokesmen for a "theology of hope" or "theology of the future," he writes:

> What lends meaning to history? The promise of the future. If there is no promise, there is no meaningful history. Significance is contingent on vision and anticipation, on living the future in the present tense.[15]

But this emphasis upon the future is not, in Heschel, in any way antithetical to an appreciation of the past. On the contrary, he asserts: "Man cannot live without a future. Man cannot live significantly without the past."[16] Nor is Heschel oversanguine about the prospects of radical alteration of the human condition in any foreseeable historical period. Jewish experience throughout the ages has been too tragic to encourage such expectations. Rather, the hope is that the worst effects of man's inhumanity to man can be avoided; the miracle is that history continues at all. The world, says Heschel, is like the burning bush, "aflame with hatred, envy, and murder—yet the world is not consumed."[17]

The Messianic hope, then, for Heschel, is a vision that hovers over history but never comes fully or finally to rest within it. Within history, we live in terms of the *deus absconditus,* whose ways are past tracing out. Even the establishment of the State of Israel, therefore, though it so clearly fulfills an age-old Jewish hope, cannot be regarded as in itself Messianic in nature. It does, however, provide what amounts to a "sign of the Kingdom"—in Heschel's words, a "solemn intimation" of God's trace in history, a "profound indication" of the possibility of redemption for all men. "The State of Israel is not the fulfillment of the Messianic promise," he concludes, "but it makes the Messianic promise plausible."[18]

In taking this position, Heschel realizes that he is having to thread his way between alternative interpretations of the Messianic hope in Jewish thought, one of which does interpret it in terms of wholly secular and even political redemption. The prophetic analysis of the human condition, however, he asserts, was too thoroughgoing to permit a solution to be propounded on that level. Judaism eventually saw the rise of apocalyptic thought, which looked not for a political solution but for a radical transformation of the world, of history, and of human nature as such.

However, Heschel is equally insistent that the Messianic hope does not absolve man of the responsibility for historical action. We may not know how to solve the problem of *evil,* he remarks, but this does not exempt us from dealing with *evils.*[19] As he puts it in *Israel:* "Not only is redemption a necessity for man, man is a necessity to redemption. His actions are vital and affect the course of that process."[20]

Abraham Heschel as a Jewish thinker thus does not share the fear of "synergism" that has caused many Christians, especially Protestants, to minimize man's role in the historical process. On the contrary, he emphasizes the "both-and" at every point. This is the import of his basic affirmation that "God is in need of man." In *Man Is Not Alone,* he quotes the following from a rabbinic commentary: "The impious rely on their gods ... the righteous are the support of God."[21] Heschel's conception, however, does not seem to be that of an *additive* relationship between God and man but, rather, of a *coinherence* of divine and human efforts. He himself uses the term "reciprocity"; and he sees such reciprocity as the meaning of the covenant, a concept which is central to biblical faith. A covenant implies a mutual commitment. It conveys an image of life as a partnership of God and man.

At this point we may return to our question of what it means to be truly human, and offer still another answer, which is implicit in what has just been said: *to be human is to share God's concern.* This theme runs throughout Heschel's writings. It is another way of stating the basic notion of a "religion of sympathy," reflective of the divine pathos.

The word "concern," however, is ambiguous. I can be concerned (or troubled, or anxious) about something that threatens me. This is what Heschel calls "reflexive" concern. Or I can be concerned about others and their welfare. This is "transitive" concern. It is the latter, of course, which characterizes God. God is in search of man because he is concerned about man; to be truly human is to share this transitive concern. Here is another aspect of the *imitatio.*

Heschel's thought provides an intriguing contrast with Tillich's at this point. Tillich speaks of God as man's ultimate concern. Heschel speaks of man as God's ultimate concern.

> God in Himself, His Being, is a problem for metaphysics. The theme and claim of prophetic theology is God's concern for man, and man's relevance to God ...
>
> ... Prophetic religion may be defined, not as what man does with his ultimate concern, but rather *what man does with God's concern.* [22]

In Heschel's volume *Who is Man?* many of the themes summarized above from his earlier work are given a fresh restatement. It may at some points have been unclear whether some of our assertions (e. g., "to be human means to share God's concern") have referred to an empirical or a normative view of man, i.e., to man as he is or as he ought to be. In *Who is Man?* the distinction is clear. "Human being" is our biologically given existence. "Being human" (the phrase used in the title of the present chapter) is a value concept; it signifies true fulfillment of our highest potentialities in accordance with the will of Him who has created us.

It is only with reference to man, as Heschel points out, that such a distinction becomes of crucial importance. It is only he who knows the "conflict between existence and expectation," and who can become so confused about the intended purpose of his being. "Man," Heschel remarks. "is endowed with an amazing degree of receptivity, conformity, and gullibility." His own self-image, distorted as it may be, becomes a factor in determining his destiny: "We become what we think of ourselves. [23]

Heschel's procedure in seeking the meaning of being human, as a normative conception, strikes one as similar to his procedure in exploring the question of God. The assumption seems to be that we all do have an inchoate knowledge, or rudimentary awareness, of what "being human" means, but this is beclouded by inherited prejudices and preconceptions and by the callousness induced by a sensate civilization. The procedure is to peel away these veils and thus come closer to the pristine awareness. "Revelation" is a process of such unveiling, and the historic wisdom about man gives guidance for our understanding of man's situation today. Heschel's procedure, then, might be defined as *phenomenological analysis in the light of prophetic faith.*

The third chapter of Heschel's book presents the concentrated results of such an analysis. He suggests the following "essential modes of being human": preciousness, uniqueness, opportunity, nonfinality, the power to create events, the polarity between solitude and solidarity, reciprocity, and sensitivity to the sacred.

Preciousness. By this, Heschel means to signify the special dignity and inviolability that we sense in the human person as contrasted with all other entities, whether animate or inanimate, that we encounter. If I do not sense this in others, I should at least sense it in myself. Indeed, such a sense for the dignity of one's own being is the foundation of morality. "The challenge I face is how to actualize, how to concretize the quiet eminence of my being." The fundamental moral question, Heschel suggests, is not "What ought I to do?" but "How should I live the life that I am?"

Uniqueness. Man cannot be understood simply as a part of nature, for his power of choice gives him transcendence over its regularities, its "laws." One cannot write one's autobiography in advance, Heschel observes. A human life consists in a unique series of events, "a going-on-ness that cannot be repeated." "No man is an average man," says Heschel, and no two individuals are alike. "Every human being has something to say, to think, or to do which is unprecedented."

Opportunity. By this Heschel seems to refer, in another sense, to the unpredictability of human life, as compared for example to the instinctual life of animals. Man's inner life is "a state of constantly increasing, indefinitely spreading complexity." It is on account of this indefiniteness that man has a need for guidance from moral and religious teaching—guidance through the labyrinth of his own being.

Nonfinality. Human life is subject to constant change—to deterioration as well as improvement. A given man may undertake various roles and pass through various, quite different stages in his life. "Man is rarely to be found in a definitive edition," Heschel comments. "A salient characteristic of being human is inconstancy both in behavior and in self-understanding, inability to remain what he is once and for all." In view of this, the utmost vigilance is called for over such values as may have been built into a culture or a character.

Process and events. Though life has a basis in organic processes, its true humanness consists in an incalculable series of occasions and events. Heschel has made this point before, but here he places emphasis on the active, initiating, organizing powers of the self. "To be human is to intend, to decide, to challenge, not merely to go on, to react, or to be an effect."

Solitude and solidarity. On the one hand, being human implies the capacity to stand apart, to be alone, to differ and to resist. On the other hand, human fulfillment is impossible without sharing in a community of human beings. "Human solidarity is not the product of being human; being human is the product of human solidarity." Solitude, then, should be understood not as the antithesis but as the complement of solidarity. It is a withdrawal in order to return. Genuine solitude implies "not discarding but distilling humanity."

Reciprocity. To become a person means to learn the meaning of both receiving and giving. The primary experience with which we begin our infancy, Heschel notes, is seizing and obtaining. Growth toward maturity means entry into the stage of giving and providing. "We receive continually; our very being is a gift in the form of an enigma; a breath of fresh air is inhalation of grace. Fullness of existence, personal being is achieved by what we offer in return."

Sanctity. Here Heschel refers not only to the sanctity of human life, but to all that which is sacred because it is "dear to God." The allusion is apparently chiefly to the realm of the religious, with its prohibitions and command-ments. But in a broader sense, all things are potentially sacred. Sacred and profane is not a final contrast.

All of the foregoing is intended as a contribution to "the meaning of being human." In this phrase, as Heschel points out, the term "meaning" is pivotal. Man is in quest of meaning. He is not satisfied merely with being; he insists on significant being. Therefore it is the ultimate grace that we can say not only that man is in quest of meaning, but also that "meaning is in quest of man." God is the meaning in and beyond the mystery of life, and out of his "care for being," his transitive concern, he seeks to draw man into this skein of meaning. Thus the meaning of existence is not naturally given, nor is it devised autonomously by man. It depends on our *response* to the challenge and the invitation with which life confronts us.

> Who is man? *A being in travail with God's dreams and designs,* with God's dream of a world redeemed, of reconciliation of heaven and earth, of a mankind which is truly His image, reflecting His wisdom, justice, and compassion. God's dream is not to be alone, to have mankind as a partner in the drama of continuous creation. [24]

Much theological reflection has been expended on the question of what might be meant by the biblical assertion that man is created in God's "image" and "likeness." To what factor or characteristic of man's life might this refer? Abraham Heschel insists that the image and likeness is not to be identified with any particular quality or attribute of man, whether it be his reason, speech, power, or skill. It is "the whole man and every man" who is made in God's image; and it is man in the total dynamics of his existence who is called to *image* (in the verbal sense) God's care for his creation. It is in this light that Heschel interprets the commandment in Leviticus 19:18 that was to be made central in the New Testament: "Love your neighbor as yourself." The neighbor here, he asserts, includes "not only the virtuous and the wise but also the vicious and the stupid man." This love will be an image-love of God's own love for man regardless of his merits or distinctions.[25]

Such imaging is the quintessence of the "religion of sympathy" implied by the prophetic proclamation. It is the final testimony to the preciousness of man.

IV

Religious Tradition and Contemporary Life-Style

"Man cannot live without a future. Man cannot live significantly without the past." Two great elements of existence are highlighted in this dictum by Abraham Heschel (see p. 47)—the elements of *hope* and *memory*. We have discussed the theme of hope in the preceding chapter. Now let us look at the role of memory, i.e., of religious tradition, in aiding contemporary man to find a meaningful identity and a coherent life-style. Since the particular tradition that Heschel represents is Jewish, this will require a closer study of the anatomy of Jewish worship, teaching, and observance.

In using the phrase "religious tradition," we hope to evoke the more positive connotations of this word "tradition," as contrasted with its more negative connotations in a phrase such as "traditional religion." "Traditional religion" implies—at least to the "now generation"— something that is out of date, irrelevant, and ossified. "The religious tradition" is meant to imply that which is a valued heritage, a source of strength and guidance, a much-needed means of orientation in a confusing world.

Certainly the latter is the focus of Abraham J. Heschel's interest. He polemicizes frequently against a mere mindless repetition of traditional words and practices, against ritualism and unbending legalism. His address to the 1957 Jerusalem Ideological Conference at Hebrew University in Jerusalem is courageous in this respect.[1] Speaking against the backdrop of the Israeli situation, in which the religious leaders maintain a rigid orthodoxy while multitudes of the citizenry live out their lives in wholly secular, socio-political terms, he deplores the "maximalism" which makes a *rapprochement* impossible. On the American scene, he has inveighed against the attitude that he calls "religious behaviorism"—the assumption that mere outward conformance to Jewish tradition (in dietary laws, etc.) is sufficient without inner commitment and devotion.

On the other hand, in the face of a generation which is increasingly ignorant of its religious heritage—and this is as prevalent among nominal Jews as among nominal Christians—he calls for redoubled effort to make contact once again with the tradition in its most vital sense. If need be, he is ready to ask Jews to undertake religious practices, such as the saying of daily prayers or stricter Sabbath observance, on an experimental basis. They are to undertake a "leap of action" (in contrast to the Kierkegaardian "leap of faith"), doing more than they understand—not, however, in order to rest with the mere doing, but to gain understanding. This he applies also to ethical obedience, not merely to ritual observance. It is a specifically Jewish form of Anselm's *fides quaerens intellectum.*

What is needed for fullness of religious thought and life is neither a cleaving to tradition at the expense of relevance, nor a pathetic search for relevance at the cost of an evacuation of the tradition. Rather, the tradition should be interpreted in light of modern questions, and modernity enriched by the resources of tradition. Each can serve as a creative challenge to the other. Heschel expresses this viewpoint clearly in his comments on the question of faith and reason. That, for Heschel, the deepest realities are accessible only to faith—i.e., to sensitivity, awareness, trust, and obedience—is evident from all that we have said above. But faith as such, he points out, is hardly able to interpret or communicate what it experiences. Reason, therefore, is its necessary coefficient. "Faith without reason is mute;

reason without faith is deaf," says Heschel.[2]

This notion of the relation between the religious heritage and the contemporary world seems very similar to Tillich's "method of correlation" between what he calls the existential questions and the kerygmatic answers. Heschel indeed speaks in similar language when he states on the first page of *God in Search of Man:* "Religion is an answer to man's ultimate questions. ... The primary task of philosophy of religion is to rediscover the questions to which religion is an answer."[3] And there is no reason to drive a wedge between Heschel and Tillich at this point; there are differences enough that appear as soon as they move from methodology to content. In fact, by the time Heschel is finished, having taken into account the divine initiative as proclaimed by the prophetic faith, he can almost reverse the foregoing formulation. "Well-adjusted people," Heschel remarks in his latest book, "think that faith is an answer to all human problems. In truth, however, faith is a challenge to all human answers."[4]

In either case, the correlation between tradition and modernity remains essential if the relevance of faith— whether as question or as answer—is to be seen. It is appropriate, therefore, that in the present chapter we conjoin the question of religious tradition with that of contemporary life-style, especially since one of the classic functions of religion has been the shaping of a style of life. But what is the meaning of this latter phrase, which has become almost a vogue-word?

Again, perhaps the dictionary will help us with the key word "style." We can quote only the most pertinent of many meanings:

> *style.* Manner of expressing thought, in writing or speaking ... Characteristic form or mode of composition, construction, or appearance, as in art, music, etc. ... The manner in which some action or work is performed. ... A mode of conduct or behavior; a way of living.[5]

Still other definitions deal with style in the sense of

fashion, as in clothing, or of consistency, as in spelling or typography. It is evident that the concept has its rootage in particular fields of activity, and is then applied metaphorically to life as a whole. Note several qualities that it implies: *creativity*—the ability to give form to a given body of material; *integrity*—the correspondence of outer expression with inner intent; *coherence*—the "fit" of details into a whole; and a sort of excellence that we might call *flair*. All of these are desiderata for a "style of life."

Both the opportunity and the necessity for considering this question arise from that indeterminateness or plasticity in human nature which Heschel, as we have seen, so strongly emphasizes. There are so many words and sentences that can be spelled with the alphabet of existence. The basic question, as Heschel points out in the last chapter of *Who Is Man?* is not how to find meaning in particular aspects or occasions of life, but rather, "how to shape one's total existence as a pattern of meaning."

> Is there a possibility of facing human existence as a whole from infancy to old age, or is man capable of living only in fractions, of going through moments unrelated to one another?
>
> The problem of living may be defined as a problem of reconciliation, of bringing about a *modus vivendi* for the self in relation to all that is. . . .
>
> . . . Life is clay, and character is form. How to lend shape, to bring order into the complexity of my inner and outer life? How to coordinate impulses, drives, ambitions? How to simplify the self?. . .
>
> Right living is like a work of art, the product of a vision and of a wrestling with concrete situations.[6]

Creativity, integrity, coherence, flair—one sees how pertinent these characteristics are to what Heschel has in mind. But is there actual historical evidence for life's having been shaped in such a way by religious faith?

Abraham Heschel's book *The Earth Is the Lord's* is a monument to a period when this was so. There are others, in both Jewish and Christian history; indeed, every important period has this kind of formative effect upon the quality and pattern of existence, each in its own way. But Heschel can assert of East European Judaism in the time of its efflorescence (roughly from the late Middle Ages to the Holocaust in the twentieth century) that it ranks as "the golden period in Jewish history, in the history of the Jewish soul." And the specific ground for his doing so is not the brilliance of artistic or intellectual achievements, which are usually the work of a few gifted individuals, but the degree to which authentic faith had penetrated into the "life-feeling and life-style of the people," i.e., of the entire community.[7]

The remote background of this development may be traced to the twelfth and thirteenth centuries, to the efforts of Jehudah ha-Hasid and his disciples to "democratize" the ideals of mystic piety. "By their apotheosis of simplicity, of warm faith, of humaneness, and moral devotion, they paved a highway to God for plain mortals." The invention of printing made the secret lore, the *Kabbalah* (or *Cabala*) available to all. This literature, however, conveyed a predominantly negative life-feeling: the believer lives surrounded by demonic forces, and every sin of his own adds to their power. Life is a constant struggle to subdue the evil urge and to beat back the darkness.

It was the Baal Shem Tov and his followers, says Heschel, who "banished melancholy from the soul and uncovered the ineffable delight of being a Jew."

> Jewishness was as though reborn. Bible verses, observances, customs, suddenly took on a flavor like that of new grain. A new prohibition was added: "Thou shalt not be old!" The Baal Shem rejuvenated us by a thousand years.[8]

To obey God's precepts was felt not as a burden but as a joy, indeed as a foretaste of heaven. As to the "evil urge," it is fought better by the power of a higher commitment than by a negative program of mortification, according to the Hasidim. Ecstasy, not asceticism, is the keynote.

[59]

Yet the tragic sense of life remained, too, as an underlying theme. It could hardly be otherwise, in view of the precarious situation in which the Jews of Eastern Europe lived continually. Their most characteristic chants, Heschel points out, are in a minor key. "Sorrow was their second soul, and the vocabulary of their heart consisted of one sound: *'Oy!'* And when there was more than the heart could say, their eyes would silently bear witness."9

The specific quality and charm of this form of Jewish life, states Heschel, consisted in this polarity between joy and sorrow, as well as between reason and feeling, intellectualism and mysticism. The inner richness of their being was reflected in their faces, which were not, he suggests, like an "open book," but like "a book whose pages are constantly turning." Only an extended quotation from Heschel's words, which themselves so deeply reflect the spirit of the culture, will give the reader an adequate feeling for this life-style:

> They had disdain for the rough, for the coarse, and tried to lend an inward dignity to everything they did. Not only the extraordinary days, not only the Sabbath, even their weekdays had a form. Everything was fixed according to a pattern. Nothing was casual, nothing was left to chance.
>
> The dishes to be served on certain days, the manner of putting on or removing one's shoes, the stance of one's head when walking in the street—everything was keyed to a certain style. Every part of the liturgy, every prayer, every hymn, had its own tune; every detail its own physiognomy, each object its individual stamp. Even the landscape became Jewish. . . .
>
> But they also had sufficient vitality to constantly modify the accepted pattern. New customs were continually added . . . , and the old customs enriched by nuances. . . .
>
> They were taught to care for the most distant in the most immediate, knowing that the passing is a reflection of the lasting, that tables in their humble homes may become consecrated altars, that a single deed of one man may decide the fate of all men. . . . The purpose was to ennoble the common to endow worldly things with hieratic beauty.10

In presenting Heschel's testimony to the vitality of this tradition, we do not mean to imply that in its concrete details it could or should serve as a model for a life-style today. But this East European Jewish culture does furnish us with a remarkable example of what is *meant* by a coherent style of life. As a matter of fact, even within the Jewish tradition there were other alternatives. Within the framework of his book *The Earth Is the Lord's,* Heschel deals with the major contrast between this Central and Eastern European form of Judaism, and the strain which centered first in Spain, and then, when the Jews were expelled from that country, in Western Europe. The former is known as Ashkenazic Judaism (from the Hebrew word for "Germany"), the latter as Sephardic (from the Hebrew word for "Spain"). Both represent a "forming" of existence, hence in our terms an identifiable life-style, but the Sephardic tends toward what Heschel calls "static form," the Ashkenazic toward "dynamic form." Synagogue services in the Sephardic tradition are calm and ordered, in the Ashkenazic tradition more spontaneous. In personal life, the Sephardim strove for tranquillity of soul; their ethics was full of prudence and practical wisdom. The Ashkenazic Jew was moved by a vision of perfection. "Not for him the tranquil contemplation, the gradual ascent. What he sought was boundless fervor. . . ."[11]

Still other contrasts are these: the Sephardic Jews strove for a synthesis with the surrounding Islamic culture; the Ashkenazic Jews lived in cultural isolation—and thereby were free to develop their own folkways more distinctively. Sephardic Judaism tended to rely for leadership upon a learned elite; Ashkenazic Judaism was more democratic. Sephardic literature used a classical Hebrew, Ashkenazic either Yiddish or a popular Hebrew. Moreover, the basic style was different. The Sephardim, suggests Heschel, were influenced more by the prose of the Talmud, the Ashkenazim by the lofty poetry of the prophets. As he further describes this contrast, we detect some of the sources of Abraham Heschel's own writing style:

> Sephardic books are distinguished by their strict logical arrangement. Composed according to a clear plan, every one of their details has its assigned place, and the transitions from one subject to another are clear and simple. Ashkenazic writers forego clarity for the sake of depth. The contours of their thoughts are irregular, vague, and often perplexingly entangled; their content is restless, animated by inner wrestling and a kind of baroque emotion. . . .
>
> Sephardic books are like neatly trimmed and cultivated parks, Ashkenazic writings like enchanted ancient forests. . . .[12]

The Sephardim, Heschel concludes, were kept spiritually alive by a "sense of balance," the Ashkenazim by a "sense of the immense." Both traditions, he adds, have had lasting influence and are living options to the present time. We might observe that they seem to correspond to the Apollonian and Dionysian, the more rational and the more ecstatic, forms of religiousness which have been identified quite broadly by phenomenologists and historians of religion.

The book which serves as a companion-piece to the volume we have just reviewed reveals in its very title Heschel's desire to correlate tradition with modernity—*The Sabbath: Its Meaning for Modern Man.* He develops his exposition in terms of the basic contrast between space and time, interpreting the Sabbath as a form of "holiness in time." Most of us, he asserts, are bewitched by the things of space. We fail to realize that that which is most precious meets us in the realm of time.[13] The things of space— whether material possessions, territory, the resources of nature, simple or technically complex tools—are easily subject to our control. Time, however is nonmanipulable— irreducible, unexpandable, irreversible. Its sovereignty is indeed mysterious. It comes as a gift; it cannot be coerced. Furthermore, it is shared by all alike. The portion of space that my body occupies cannot be occupied by any other, but the present moment is shared by me and all living men.

Time, says Heschel, is almost holy. Indeed, by the conclusion of his discussion he affirms explicitly, "Time is the presence of God in the world of space." It is a form of the *Shechinah.*

> When looking at space we see the products of creation; when intuiting time we hear the process of creation. Things of space exhibit a deceptive independence. They show off a veneer of limited permanence. Things created conceal the Creator. It is the dimension of time wherein man meets God, wherein man becomes aware that every instant is an act of creation, a Beginning, opening up new roads for ultimate realizations.[14]

Judaism is pre-eminently a religion of time, not space, says Heschel. This is another way of stating that it is a religion of history, not of nature. Judaism prizes sacred moments, not sacred places. Agricultural festivals are converted into celebrations of historical events. The destruction of the Temple and even expulsion from the land does not destroy the faith. Not that space and the things of space are to be disparaged. On the contrary, they represent God's good creation, and land and Temple can become exceedingly precious once again, as modern Jews have rediscovered in the return to Israel. But the things of space must not be permitted to obscure the paramount significance of time.

It is this which accounts for the importance of the Sabbath. Jewish ritual, Heschel states in a striking phrase, may be regarded as "the art of significant forms in time, as *architecture of time.*"[15] The day, the week, the year are structured. But pre-eminent is the weekly cycle, which according to the Genesis story dates to the creation itself: "And God blessed the seventh day and made it holy." The function of the Sabbath, says Heschel, is to teach us to become attuned to holiness in time.

True to his Hasidic heritage, Heschel emphasizes the element of joy rather than renunciation in Sabbath observance.

Yet he does take seriously also the abstentions, i.e., what is not to be done on that day. (For Heschel personally, the end of Sabbath is marked by the first lighting up within twenty-four hours of one of his cherished long cigars!) The purpose of these abstentions, however, is only to make room for the positive content of the day: a fervent rejoicing in God's presence, in the presence of eternity. "Rest" is far too thin a word to describe what the Sabbath is meant to bring us. The biblical term *menuha,* Heschel explains, should, rather, be rendered by such words as "tranquillity," "serenity," "peace and harmony." The term occurs in the Twenty-third Psalm: "He leads me beside the waters of *menuhot."* In later times, adds Heschel, it became a synonym for life in the world to come, or eternal life.

Abraham Heschel's use of the concepts of "eternity" and "eternal life" may surprise some who have been led to think that neither the Hebrew Bible nor later Judaism has any concerns beyond the temporal. He has had to make a corrective here, similar to his correction of the notion that Judaism is an entirely unmystical religion. In Heschel's thought, it is clear that to describe Judaism as a "religion of time" is not to deny its concern with transtemporal realities; the operative contrast here is time/space, not time/eternity.

Heschel's basic work in the philosophy of religion, *Man Is Not Alone,* contains a sensitive discussion of this question. There is no man, he asserts, who does not have, implicitly or explicitly, a craving for "something that outlasts life, strife, and agony," for that which abides beyond the dyingness of our deeds and our intentions. Attachment to the lasting is a psychological necessity—and an ontological reality. Here Heschel the phenomenologist functions again. Characteristic of existence is not only temporality, evanescence, but also continuity, "uninterruptedness." Life occurs moment by moment, but also it does "go on." This structural reality provides a clue to the meaning of eternity, which for Heschel (as also for the Hebrew Bible, according to some scholars[16]) appears to have both quantitative and qualitative connotations. It implies, on the one hand, everlastingness or immortality, and on the other hand, eschatological fulfillment.

The Sabbath, we may say, is for Heschel an *eschatological* reality. It gives us a foretaste of the world to come. It is a weekly resurrection of the soul—of the soul of man and of the soul of all things. No doubt it is this eschatological sense which accounts for the extravagant language of much Jewish Sabbath piety (language which Heschel partly repeats) concerning the Sabbath as pre-existent, or as the Queen or Bride to whom Israel is betrothed, etc. The Sabbath is a gateway to eternity. Of course, all days are meant to be such gateways. It is of God's grace that we have the Sabbath to be our tutor in this respect. In *Man Is Not Alone,* Heschel expresses this concept of the relation of time and eternity in a memorable image:

> Time is the border of eternity. Time is eternity formed into tassels. The moments of our lives are like luxuriant tassels. They are attached to the garment and are made of the same cloth. It is through spiritual living that we realize that the infinite can be confined in a measured line.[17]

A pragmatic test of the significance of this conception can be found in Heschel's lecture on the problem of aging ("To Grow in Wisdom," his address to the White House Conference of 1961[18]). He urges the elderly to continue to cultivate character and the spiritual life. The years of old age, he suggests, should still be regarded as "formative years." What sense would this make if there were not an expectation that something of the personhood of this elderly person may survive the moment of death?

Heschel's reflections on the Sabbath, it may be said in summary, can be regarded as having three levels of potential meaning for modern man. The first is at the level of the very general problem of the structuring of time, which some psychologists have suggested is *the* basic human problem. Here, of course, not only the Sabbath but other aspects of Jewish belief and ritual, too, are illustrative of the service which a religious tradition can perform in providing such a structuring. The second level is that of the problem of work and leisure, which has troubled recent theology, some maintaining that the traditional "Protestant work ethic" is outmoded by the age of automation, others that it is not. Very significant is the fact that the traditional Jewish observance of the Sabbath had as its counterpoint a very industrious life of work on the other six days. The onerousness of work heightened the joy of the Sabbath; the delights of the day of "rest" sent one refreshed back to the world of work. (It should be understood that family meals and other positive human pleasures were also a part of Sabbath observance.) We might learn from this that the ideal combination is intensive work and elevating leisure. Presumably a theology of work and a theology of leisure will both continue to be required.

The third level on which the Sabbath, as Heschel interprets it, has significance is that of the relation of time and eternity, which we have already dealt with; but we may point out the implications which he draws from it for "the problem of civilization." The problem which Heschel thus formulates is the Jewish equivalent of the "Christ and culture" issue among Christians. What attitude shall be taken toward secular civilization? An uncritical acceptance, and even a confinement of one's perspective to this secular horizon? To take such an attitude would be to betray the eschatological significance of the Sabbath, the precious "more" that it provides. On the other hand, a hypercritical disparagement or rejection of civilization would be a denial of the divine commandment and permission to "subdue the earth," the daily work which occupies the remainder of the week. Civilization is not inherently evil, nor is it adequate in itself. "The Sabbath," writes Heschel, "is the day on which we learn the art of *surpassing* civilization." In *Israel,* he puts it this way: man's task is "not to abandon the natural order of creation but to purify it."[19]

The clue to living in the midst of modern technical civilization without losing one's integrity, Heschel suggests, is not to renounce technical civilization, but to attain some degree of independence from it. "In regard to external gifts, to out-ward possessions, there is only one proper attitude—to have them and to be able to do without them."[20] This sounds remarkably like a restatement—somewhat more positive in its orientation, to be sure—of Paul's "having as having not" in I Corinthians 7. ("Let those who have wives live as though they had none, . . . and those who buy as though they had no goods. . . . ") Doubtless such an attitude is bound to result when one combines the basic Judeo-Christian faith in the goodness of creation with the ecstasy of eschatological fulfillment—whether it be through the Queen Sabbath or the King Messiah.

V

Worship, Learning, Action

(There are three routes, says Abraham J. Heschel, to an awareness of God's presence, three ways in which the heart that seeks him may truly find him. "The first is the way of sensing the presence of God in the world, in things; the second is the way of sensing His presence in the Bible; the third is the way of sensing His presence in sacred deeds."[1] These three ways correspond to the three great facets of religious existence as experienced by Judaism: worship, learning, and action. We want to review some of Heschel's contributions in each of these three areas.)

The first involves Heschel's concept of the nature and role of prayer, a topic which not every theologian has ventured to deal with in this day of "death-of-God" theologies, but which for Heschel is fundamental. The conception of the Living God, deeply concerned with human affairs and hiddenly involved in all of history, whose pathos changes in response to changing situations—of Him who is not an unmoved Mover but the *most moved* Mover, ready for reciprocity with the believing man—all this suggests that prayer is not only possible but necessary for the life of faith. For man lives not in terms of a naturally unfolding process, but by decisions and events, and his fullest humanness is shown not in dumb passivity but in articulateness and awareness. Prayer is the raising of the divine-human relationship to this level of articulateness and awareness.

[68]

The predominant mood of Jewish prayer and liturgy, as is well known, is that of praise: the adoration of God, thanksgiving for his benefits, the celebration of his mighty deeds. The sequence of themes in the famous "Eighteen Benedictions," the *Amidah,* is typical. The first two, as rendered in a recent translation, are as follows:[2]

> Blessed are you, O Lord our God and God of our Fathers, God of Abraham, God of Isaac, and God of Jacob, the God who is great, strong, and awesome, the most high God; who bestows goodness, and owns all things, and remembers the goodness of the fathers, and will bring a redeemer to their children's children, for his name's sake, in love. King, helper, savior, shield!
> *Blessed are you, O Lord, shield of Abraham.*
> You are powerful for ever O Lord, quickener of the dead, mighty to save. You support life with kindness, quicken the dead with great mercy. You raise the fallen, heal the sick, free the prisoned, and keep faith with those that sleep in the dust. Who is like you, master of mighty acts, and who compares to you? O King who kills and who brings to life, and who makes salvation flower, faithful are you to give life to the dead.
> *Blessed are you, O Lord, who give life to the dead.*

Only after such lavish praise does the prayer move on to petition, and it is petition first not for physical needs but for understanding, the spirit of repentance, and forgiveness. The prayer ends with a return once more to the note of thanksgiving: "We thank you, for you are the Lord our God, the rock of our lives, the shield of our salvation, from generation to generation. We will thank you and we will tell your praise. . . ."

This emphasis on praise accords very well with Heschel's thought; or, rather, let us say that his thought has succeeded well in transcribing this spirit of prayer, for the latter is primary. Praise is the natural expression of the radical amazement, wonder, awe, appreciation, which Heschel finds at the root of faith. And as he reminds us, such a sense is not given once for all. It needs to be cultivated. Hence the need for continually repeated acts of worship and prayer.

The accent is in the first instance on what prayer does for man: it permits him to express and deepen his sense of wonder, his contrition, his sense of need, and his concern for the concerns of God. But it can also affect the cosmos and the Creator himself. This conviction, as Heschel demonstrates, is fundamental to both the mystical and the prophetic traditions. The Jewish mystics were convinced that "There is always a reverberation in the Beyond to every action here." Their aim was to become "allied with the dynamics of secret worlds."[3] Likewise the prophets declared "the extreme pertinence of man to God," the fact that God " 'looks at' the world and is affected by what happens in it."[4] And the prophets themselves pleaded most fervently with God, hoping to influence his response.

Heschel's most extended treatment of prayer is contained in the first three chapters of his book *Man's Quest for God,* where he offers many variations on the themes indicated above. Prayer is "the opening of our thoughts to God." We cannot make God visible to us, but in prayer we can make ourselves visible to him. Prayer is "our humble answer to the inconceivable surprise of living." It is "arrival at the border." Prayer assumes man's ability to accost God, to lay our concerns before him. But this itself is God's gift; in reality, since God is in search of man, prayer is only the clearing of the path for his approach. The purpose of prayer is "to be brought to His attention, to be listened to, to be understood by Him; not to know Him, but to *be known* to Him." The man who prays, says Heschel, thereby expresses his aspiration "to be thought of by God as one who is thinking of Him."[5]

The quality of a man's prayer, says Heschel, depends on the quality of his life. *Kavanah,* inner participation or devotion, is essential. This does not mean, however, that the use of a fixed form of words, as in the synagogue service, is ineffectual or inauthentic. Heschel distinguishes between two types of prayer: prayer as an "act of expression" and as an "act of empathy." In the former, the intention and the desire to pray come first, and the words follow. In the latter type, the words come first and the feeling follows; by empathy with the given text, our capacity to pray expands. Both are essential; this only reflects the tension between regularity and spontaneity, *keva* and *kavanah,* that obtains throughout the realm of religious observance. The problem is to ensure that the factor of regularity, e.g., the repetition of liturgical forms, does not stifle the spirit of spontaneity, while at the same time the principle of spontaneity does not undermine the disciplined regularity of prayer.

One of the greatest treasures of the Jewish tradition is its heritage of benedictions—not only the Eighteen Benedictions cited above, but innumerable forms of blessing, both prescribed and to be spontaneously devised, upon all sorts of occasions in life. To Heschel this is very meaningful. It is a way of maintaining the sense of the ineffable.

> Wishing to eat bread or fruit, to enjoy a pleasant fragrance or a cup of wine; on tasting fruit in season for the first time; on seeing a rainbow, or the ocean; on noticing trees when they blossom; on meeting a sage in Torah or in secular learning; on hearing good or bad tidings—we are taught to invoke His great name and our awareness of Him. [6]

To pray, Heschel declares, is to expand God's presence in the world. It is "to establish His kingship, to let His glory prevail." God is transcendent; our worship makes him immanent. [7]

It is interesting to note that, for all his stress upon God's initiative and his pathos, Heschel resists the concept of prayer as dialogue, or as analogous to a conversation between persons. "Who are we to enter a dialogue with God?" he asks. The better metaphor, he suggests, would be that of immersion, like the ancient Hebrew custom of ritual purifications. "Immersion in the waters! One feels surrounded, touched by the waters, drowned in the waters of mercy." [8] For this reason, Heschel rejects the "I-Thou" terminology; he prefers "it-He." The consciousness of the "I" recedes, while the awareness grows of being an "it," an object in the thought of

God. Prayer is a movement from self-consciousness to self-surrender.[9]

"Learning" is the second great factor in Jewish existence, corresponding to Heschel's second way to God— "the way of sensing his presence in the Bible." It is revealing that this word is thus applied as a technical term to the study of the Scriptures, though it could in principle have any content whatsoever. For Orthodox Judaism and especially for Hasidism, the only learning worth having was sacred learning; and Heschel himself was reared in this tradition. Later, he broke free from its exclusiveness, but he remained the beneficiary of the intensity and intimacy of study of the Scriptures that characterized the Hasidic schools. One of his chief conclusions after a period spent in the sophisticated circles of the University of Berlin, he reports in an autobiographical statement,[10] was that "There is much that philosophy could learn from Jewish life"—i.e., from the Bible, and from its reverberation in Jewish faith and practice. Heschel's career may be seen as an effort to recover and revivify for contemporary man the basic categories of biblical thought.

In doing so, he has had to struggle on two fronts, as have Christian theologians: on the one hand, against an orthodoxy which clings to the text in a wooden manner, and on the other hand, against a modernism that loses all sense for the uniqueness of biblical revelation. One does not find major attention devoted to the former struggle in Heschel's writings, though it it does come to expression from time to time. He rejects theories of direct dictation to the prophets, the failure to realize the symbolic character of many biblical expressions, and an undiscriminating adherence to the entire corpus of Mosaic law. His major struggle, however, is against the modern disinclination to accept any form of revelation at all.

Modern thought has alternately regarded man as either too exalted to need any such infusion of guidance or wisdom, or else as too lowly to deserve it. Likewise God has been regarded as either too removed from the world-process or too simply identified with it to be able to "speak" to man. All these notions Heschel combats, especially in the middle chapters of *God in Search of Man,* which are devoted to this theme. He further criticizes the historian Leopold von Ranke's dictum that "every age is equidistant from God." On the contrary, Heschel asserts, according to Jewish faith there is a "hierarchy of moments within time." God is *not* equally available or equally communicative at all times. Therefore we must prize the specific moments of revelation, and the record of such moments. "Sinai does not happen every day, and prophecy is not a perpetual process."[11]

It is foolish to despise the Bible as old and therefore out-dated. In fact, states Heschel, it is still at the very beginning of its career, the full meaning of its content having hardly begun to dawn upon us. Yet its influence already in the history of civilization has been remarkable. It is the fountain-head of the finest strivings of Western man.

> The Bible is mankind's greatest privilege. It is so far off and so direct, categorical in its demands and full of compassion in its understanding of the human situation. No other book so loves and respects the life of man. No loftier songs about his true plight and glory, about his agony and joys, misery and hope, have ever been expressed, and nowhere has man's need for guidance and the certainty of his ultimate redemption been so keenly conceived. It has the words that startle the guilty and the promise that upholds the forlorn. And he who seeks a language in which to utter his deepest concern, to pray, will find it in the Bible.[12]

It is evident that Heschel's conception of the authority of the Bible is that of an *intrinsic* authority—its actual power to persuade, to unveil, to instruct. There is no need for a heteronomous concept of revelation.

The Bible does not exist in the abstract, however. It is given to a community, the community of Israel. Heschel can define the specific calling of the Jewish people in this way: "to be a community in which the Bible lives on." But this raises the question of whether the community which is the custodian of the Bible does not affect or shape its influence in a substantial way by virtue of its role in the interpretation of the text. Heschel acknowledges that this is indeed so; he is more "Catholic" than "Protestant" at this point. "We approach the laws of the Bible through the interpretation and the wisdom of the Rabbis. . . . The prophets' inspirations and the sages' interpretations are equally important."[13] Yet the Bible retains the initiating role. Heschel expresses the coinherence of Scripture and tradition in words which a Christian might well ponder, substituting the word "church" for "Israel": "Just as in the words of the Bible history became Scripture, so in the life of Israel Scripture became history."[14]

Both because of the primacy of the Bible and because of the dynamic character of the life of faith, Heschel assigns only limited significance to doctrinal or dogmatic formulations. They can serve to express genuine insight; on the other hand, they can obscure it. Heschel is far from accepting the proposition that Judaism has no dogmas. Beginning from the belief in the oneness of God and extending to the resurrection from the dead, it most certainly has. However, they retain an instrumental function. "The adequacy of dogmas depends upon whether they claim to formulate or to allude; in the first case they flaunt and fail, in the second they indicate and illumine." Dogmas, Heschel suggests, properly have a "telescopic" character: they point to the mysteries of God rather than picture them.[15]

It appears to be on account of the dogmatic connotations involved that Heschel for the most part avoids the use of the word "theology" for his own work, unless it be in the phrase "depth theology." No doubt this latter phrase was suggested to him by the term "depth psychology" (as contrasted with a more superficial behaviorism), as well as Tillich's popularization of the notion of the "depth dimension" of existence. By depth theology, Heschel means an approach which deals with the level of direct experience of the divine, not merely the level of conceptualization; with the act of believing more than the content of belief. Theology in the usual sense declares; depth theology evokes. Theology abstracts and generalizes; depth theology prizes spontaneity and uniqueness. Conceptual theology, Heschel concludes, is not unnecessary, but neither is it adequate. What is essential is to preserve the sense of "the incongruity of dogma and mystery."[16]

The third way to God, in addition to worship and learning, that Heschel identifies is the way of action—the dimension of the deed. To Christian, and especially Protestant, ears it may sound rather strange that action is spoken of as a route *to* faith rather than a derivative from it. We think of faith active in love, in that order. Heschel, however, suggests that the venture of obedience to a concrete command (*mitzvah*) may in itself serve to quicken the sense of God's reality, and hence permit a faith-response. This may not in fact be so distant from the Christian view. One thinks of the New Testament text, "if any man's will is to do His will, he shall know whether the teaching is from God . . ." (John 7:17).

The specifics of the discussion in Heschel, however, are very much oriented to the particularly Jewish problem of the nature and scope of religious law. We have already noted that he, on the one hand, rejects a "maximalist" conception, i.e., any kind of fundamentalist attitude toward the Mosaic Code. On the other hand, he urges the contemporary Jew who may be estranged from the tradition to "do more than he understands in order to understand more than he does."[17] To use terms more familiar from the Christian discussion, neither legalism nor antinomianism is the answer.

For Heschel, this *via media* is expressed in terms of the distinction commonly made between the two great components of the Talmudic literature—the legal and the nonlegal elements, *halacha* and *haggada* (or *agada*) respectively. In some periods of Jewish life, the former has been the almost exclusive focus of attention. But the *haggada* is equally important. Taking the literary form not of statutes but of Scriptural expositions and homilies, rabbinic tales, folk wisdom, historical reminiscences, and ethical reflections, it represents the elements of inwardness and spontaneity in religion which, as we know, Heschel esteems so highly. Both *halacha* and *haggada* are essential in the life of faith. Indeed, they can only survive in symbiosis. "To reduce Judaism to law, to halacha," writes Heschel, "is to dim its light, to pervert its essence and to kill its spirit." On the other hand, "To reduce Judaism to inwardness, to agada, is to blot out its light, to dissolve its essence and to destroy its reality."[18]

It is striking that Heschel's discussion of "the way of action" is primarily personal, not to say individualistic, in its reference. The dimension of the social and political, of large-scale questions of public policy, is dealt with, rather, in connection with his exposition of the prophets. The law implies for the Jew, in the first instance, a very personal level of action or abstention. It deals with such things as the consumption of food and drink, the rhythm of work and leisure, the virtues of kindness and self-control—some of which may seem rather small-scale problems when compared with the great burning issues of the day. But it is in dealing responsibly with small things, Heschel reminds us, that we learn to deal responsibly with great ones; and it is private faithfulness that undergirds public integrity. Furthermore, this ethical *via negationis* may prove to be, in fact, the route to personal fulfillment. "Self-respect is the fruit of discipline," Heschel asserts; "the sense of dignity grows with the ability to say No to oneself."[19]

"Discipline" is not a word that sits well with the contemporary generation. Heschel, however, in his address to the White House Conference on Children and Youth, made bold to ask whether it really is an obsolescent concept in an affluent society, as is claimed. Basic to being human, according to the religious tradition, is an acknowledgment of one's indebtedness. The question, said Heschel—antedating John F. Kennedy's similar formula in his Inaugural Address—is not what I will get out of life, but what will life, what will society, get out of me? But to be of service in this larger context requires the curbing of one's private "needs," which if unchecked prove so imperious. As Heschel puts it in *Who Is Man?*: "Human being is boundless, but being human is respect for bounds."[20]

None of this should be taken as indicative of a negative attitude toward the bodily as such. Heschel is very clear on this point. In fact, he suggests that it is the part of wisdom "to please the natural needs of the flesh so that the spirit should not be molested by unnatural frustrations."[21] Yet, on the other hand, Heschel is vividly aware of the power of rationalization so to exaggerate the legitimacy of one's own desires that one becomes quite blind to their destructiveness. For this reason the guidance of a religious and ethical tradition is essential. The proper course is "neither to deify nor to vilify" the flesh, but to seek its proper fulfillment in the context of a total fulfillment of oneself and of the community. A purely self-centered approach is not only wrong but futile, for man cannot be man, Heschel affirms, unless he surpasses himself. "This is the profound paradox and redeeming feature of human existence. There is no joy for the self within the self. Joy is found in giving rather than acquiring; in serving rather than in taking."[22] It is tragic that the widespread loss today of a sense of requiredness in face of an objective moral order, and of being needed by a transcendent God and called to share his concerns, is robbing so many of the present generation of this deeper dimension of their selfhood.

A discussion of "the way of action" as guided by divine commandments inevitably raises the question of whether man does have the capacity to do the good. We noted in a previous chapter (see p. 43) that although he is very cognizant of man's fallenness, in the sense of his distorted and diminished humanity, indeed his inhumanity, Heschel does not have any formal "doctrine of the Fall." The same holds true here. His consciousness of man's sinfulness, both at the private and at the public level, is very strong, and he urges on the believer the attitude of continual repentance and constant struggle against the "evil drive." "Life is a spiritual battlefield," Heschel writes. He quotes from a medievalist, "Man is like unto a rope, one end of which is pulled by God and the other end by Satan."[23] Yet he maintains that man does have the ability to fulfill what God demands, "at least to some degree."[24]

In an important essay contributed to the volume on the thought of Reinhold Niebuhr published in the "Library of Living Theology" in 1956,[25] Heschel expresses profound appreciation for the contributions of his friend and neighbor at Union Theological Seminary. "In boldness of penetration, depth of insight, fullness of vision and comprehensiveness, Reinhold Niebuhr's system excels everything which the whole of American theology has hitherto produced," he writes.[26] Heschel considers that Niebuhr has helped to recover for modern America some of the essential insights of prophetic thinking. Among these is a very realistic sense of evil—and not only of evil, but of the mysterious intertwining of good and evil in man's history. Heschel finds a striking parallel to Niebuhr's view in a comment of the Baal Shem on this verse from Ezekiel: "For there is not a righteous man upon this earth that does good and sins not." Most of the rabbinic commentators, Heschel notes, take this to mean that even a righteous man sins *on occasion.* But the Baal Shem interprets it as meaning: "There is not a righteous man upon earth that does good and there is no sin in the good"—i.e., that the "confusion of good and evil" infects even the best of actions.[27] Yet Heschel warns against concluding from this that sin is inevitable.

Over against what he takes to be Niebuhr's fatalism on this score (though Niebuhr surely would reject the charge), Heschel asserts that Jewish tradition stresses "man's actual failures rather than his essential inability to do the good."[28] To be sure, one's motives are never perfect, but it is not essential to have full purity of motivation in order to do good. The purification of motive can take place in and through the action. "While insisting on the contrast between God's power and man's power, God's grace and human failure," Heschel writes, "Judaism stresses a third aspect, the *mitzvah*. It is a *mitzvah* that gives meaning to our existence. The *mitzvah*, the carrying out of a sacred deed, is given to us as a constant opportunity."[29] Worship, learning, action—all are routes to God's reality and to man's fulfillment.

VI

Encounter between
Christianity and Judaism

The twentieth century has been an epochal period both for Judaism itself and for the relationship between Judaism and Christianity. For Judaism, it has brought within the space of a few short years both unspeakable disaster and unparalleled blessing. The disaster: the annihilation of six million European Jews. The blessing: the return to the Jewish homeland after almost two thousand years of exile. Since the day the Temple was destroyed, says Abraham Heschel, there has been no age like this. "It is as if God had rolled up all Jewish history and placed it under our heads."[1] In these two events—the Holocaust and the Return—are revealed the satanic and the sublime, the wonder and the horror at the heart of history, the grandeur and the misery of being a Jew.

Likewise these recent decades have been momentous for Jewish-Christian relations. Again, there is a darker and a brighter side. On the one hand, the tragic developments in Germany and German-dominated Europe could with some historical justice be seen as the culmination of the long and dismal story of anti-Semitism within Christendom. True, the Nazis set their faces against prophetic Christianity as well, and might more properly be regarded as neo-pagans than as heirs of Christendom. But how many Christians saw the matter thus, and deeply felt and acted on their kinship with the Jews? Blessed be God for the minority who did!

Even today, however, and even in America, there are signs that this cancerous growth within Western civilization—for anti-Semitism is a sign of illness in the whole body politic[2]—still lingers on. With regard to this, every Christian and every sensitive American will be moved to say a *mea culpa;* for as Abraham Heschel has said regarding the analogous problem of antiblack discrimination: "Some are guilty, but all are responsible."[3]

On the positive side, the present century has seen also the development of remarkably open human and theological relationships between Christianity and Judaism. Whatever may be said about the hackneyed rhetoric of "Brotherhood Week," in the light of history it is an achievement not to be despised that Jews and Gentiles should have learned to live together in toleration, mutual respect, and a full sharing in both the rights and the duties of citizenship; and as we have suggested, this is a legacy to be guarded carefully. Even more remarkable, however, is the *theological* openness that has developed between the two traditions. The most visible sign of this, no doubt, is the widespread influence within Christian theology of Martin-Buber and his concept of "I-Thou" relations. But there are other, perhaps less-well-known areas of interaction too. Paul Tillich, in an invaluable essay on "Jewish Influences on Contemporary Christian Theology,"[4] reviews the following areas in which he finds the influence of Jewish thought and scholarship to be significant: biblical archeology and textual criticism; studies in the historical and ideological background of the New Testament; research in early Christian history, especially in the early "Jewish Christianity"; the reconsideration of the relation between mysticism and the biblical tradition; studies in the role of religious art and symbolism; and the whole area of eschatology, with its decisive implications for the relationship of ethical and sacramental elements in religion. "In our period," Tillich asserts, "something is going on between Jewish and Christian thought which has not happened since the two religions parted in life, thought and destiny in the first and second centuries."[5]

Abraham Heschel, in his inaugural lecture as Harry Emerson Fosdick Visiting Professor at Union Theological Seminary in New York—an appointment which was itself indicative of this interaction—agrees with this judgment. He notes a receptivity in the Christian world for Jewish insights. And speaking as a Jew, he expresses also the Jewish indebtedness to Christianity, not only for recent contributions such as the work of the great Protestant Old Testament (Heschel says simply: biblical) scholars, but also for Christianity's historic role in spreading the knowledge of the God of Abraham and the Hebrew Scriptures among the nations of mankind. Furthermore, Jewish literary products such as the Septuagint, the Apocrypha and Pseudepigrapha, and the works of Philo and Josephus would have been lost to the world, Heschel notes, if they had not been preserved in Christian monasteries. And as to the great heritage of Christian theology and philosophy, he asks: "Have not Pascal, Kierkegaard, Immanuel Kant or Reinhold Niebuhr been a source of inspiration to many Jews?"[6]

The present study of the promise of Abraham Joshua Heschel may be regarded as an effort to make a small contribution to this process of mutual fructification. But it may be asked, Is Heschel truly representative of Judaism? This is an important and delicate question. As is well known, Judaism has no Pope, no curia, no authoritative teaching office, and no one is chartered to speak for the whole of Jewry on a given question. Furthermore, there are the manifest differences in ritual observance and mode of worship, as well as biblical and theological interpretation, that underlie the distinction between Orthodox, Conservative, and Reform movements or "denominations" in American Judaism. In this sense, the answer to our question must be No. Neither Heschel nor any other single theologian is "representative" of Judaism.

But in another sense, Heschel *is* highly representative,

insofar as he recapitulates within himself so many aspects of the Jewish tradition. He is an expositor of the Hebrew Bible; a Talmudic scholar; a student of Maimonides; an expert on medieval mysticism; an heir of the Hasidic movement; and a voice of the modern Jewish social conscience. Well might a spokesman for the Rabbinical Assembly, when that body at its meeting in March, 1968, paid tribute to Professor Heschel on the occasion of his sixtieth birthday, assert that "Abraham Heschel is one of the few authentic Jews of our time," noting that "he has been able to speak to and influence every segment of Jews today."[7] The stature and scope of Heschel's thought have also been stressed in reviews and articles by such Jewish scholars as Will Herberg, Emil Fackenheim, Maurice Friedman, Jakob Petuchowski, and Jacob Neusner, and he is given major attention in two recent books surveying modern Jewish thought: Arthur A. Cohen's *The Natural and the Supernatural Jew* and Eugene B. Borowitz's *A New Jewish Theology in the Making.*[8]

These expositions are not uncritical. The most frequent charge brought against Heschel's work is that it relies more on rhetoric than on logic, moving the reader with vivid imagery rather than leading him carefully through the steps of an argument. In answer, it has been pointed out that Heschel's poetic style is helpful and even essential to his purpose of awakening new levels of sensitivity, and that his more *haggadic* style is appropriate to an age which, if Marshall McLuhan is correct, is moving into a "post-linear" phase. Heschel has been criticized from the liberal side as being semifundamentalist in his view of biblical authority, while from the side of orthodoxy, he has been charged with taking undue liberties with the tradition.[9] All agree, however, that Abraham Joshua Heschel is a major voice to be reckoned with in the contemporary Jewish world.

Among Christian theologians, special attention has been given to Heschel's thought by Professor Edmond LaB. Cherbonnier of Trinity College, Hartford, as well as by

Reinhold Niebuhr, who was one of the first to call attention to his "rare gifts as poet, mystic, and interpreter of Biblical thought."[10] Fortunately, it has not happened with Heschel as in some other instances that a Jewish thinker who is warmly received by Christians has difficulty maintaining his standing in his own community. Even Martin Buber had this experience, it seems, due largely to his negative attitude toward Jewish ritual and law. With Heschel this is not the case; even as his influence in broader circles grows, he remains firmly implanted in Jewish observance, and firmly attached to congregational life. Not that he is uncritical of Judaism in America. A review of his addresses to Jewish rabbis, cantors, and educationists reveals a critique of Jewish religiousness quite equal in its severity to that which Protestant and Roman Catholic critics have leveled at their own households of faith in recent years. In the face of widespread biblical illiteracy, the preoccupation of many rabbis with public relations or with the running of organizational machinery, and the decline of Jewish observance in the home, Heschel can go so far as to assert that "Judaism today is an unknown religion." He is particularly scornful of the notion that "Judaism has no theology," which he traces back to Spinoza's dismissal of the *intellectual* relevance of the Bible. Even among Jews, Heschel observes, the grand heritage of Jewish thought "has been kept a well-guarded secret."[11]

The word "religion," as the reader may have observed, has been used in our exposition of Heschel's thought primarily in a positive sense, a usage that may have seemed naive to those who are *au courant* with recent discussion, inspired largely by Bonhoeffer, of the need to go "beyond religion," or of the "disappearance of the religious premise" from the life of modern man. There is room for a good deal of misunderstanding here. Much that Bonhoeffer labeled "religion" would be rejected by Judaism also, under the label of "idolatry." Heschel is well aware of the prophetic anger that declares, "I hate, I despise your feasts," and it should be clear from material such as that cited in the preceding paragraph that he gives no blanket endorsement to what goes on in churches or in synagogues. As a matter of fact Heschel himself, in a major utterance on the subject, makes the distinction between religion in the positive (or neutral) sense, and "religion" (in quotes) of the sort that is, indeed, dispensable:

> Little does contemporary religion ask of man. It is ready to offer comfort; it has no courage to challenge. It is ready to offer edification; it has no courage to break the idols, to shatter callousness. The trouble is that religion has become "religion"— institution, dogma, ritual. . . .
> . . . When faith is completely replaced by creed, worship by discipline, love by habit; when the crisis of today is ignored because of the splendor of the past; when faith becomes an heirloom rather than a living fountain; when religion speaks only in the name of authority rather than with the voice of compassion, its message becomes meaningless.[12]

It is significant that when the *Christian Century* published an issue in December, 1963, devoted to the question "Is Protestantism Reformable?" Abraham J. Heschel was asked to be among the contributors. He strikes at once to the theological heart of the issue. The malaise of contemporary Protestantism, he suggests, is attributable above all to two factors: what he calls the "dejudaization of Christianity" and the "desanctification of the Hebrew Bible."

On the former issue, which as Heschel points out represents an age-old process, the reader is struck with the frankness and incisiveness of Heschel's analysis, which duplicates that made by many Christian historians and theologians. Christianity, he points out, originally considered itself to be an affirmation and culmination of Judaism, but it soon became diverted into a repudiation and negation of Judaism. Not its indebtedness to, but its divergencies from, its mother-faith were stressed. "The children did not arise and call the mother blessed; instead, they called the mother blind." Judaism was billed as a religion of law, Christianity as a religion of grace. Judaism taught a God of wrath, Christianity a God of love. Judaism was the religion of slavery, Christianity a religion of freedom; Judaism particularistic, Christianity universalistic; Judaism based on works-righteousness, Christianity on faith-righteousness. Judaism was based on fear, Christianity on love.[13]

The result of the overdrawing of these contrasts was not only that Christians alienated themselves from the Jewish people, but also, Heschel makes bold to say, that they lost the capacity to understand their own faith correctly. "The vital issue for the church," writes Heschel, "is to decide whether to look for roots in Judaism and consider itself an extension of Judaism or to look for roots in pagan Hellenism and consider itself as an antithesis to Judaism." [14]

The second fateful process identified by Heschel is the desanctification of the Bible, i.e., the loss of the conviction of its authority. Heschel refers particularly to the Hebrew Bible (the Old Testament), but the same applies, for modern Protestantism, to the New Testament. The Bible, according to liberal scholarship, was to be treated "like any other book." But, insists Heschel, the Bible is *not* just like any other book, just as my own mother is not just like any other mother to me. The Bible is the very root of our religious life. It is "holiness in words." And to study it requires not only scholarly preparation but openness to the divine presence. Torah in the sense of specific revelation is indispensable. The word of the Lord in Jeremiah concerning the law to be written upon men's hearts, Heschel suggests, does not imply abolition of the Torah so much as inner identification with it.

In concluding his article on Protestant renewal, Heschel returns to his familiar theme of the need to concentrate not on dogmatic formulations, which can do no more than allude to the mystery, but on the deeper levels of insight and commitment. The renewal of religion takes place in the context of new and urgent problems facing mankind as such. Essential, says Heschel, is an awareness that "The greater problem today is not how to preserve the church but how to preserve humanity."[15]

What shall we say to these things, speaking from the Christian standpoint? Taking Heschel's points in reverse order, the last-named, the emphasis on social relevance, is most welcome. As to the role of dogma, we can agree also, on the understanding that Heschel is not dismissing it entirely but only trying to keep it in perspective. In this very essay, he fully acknowledges its role—like that of formulated law—in helping "to communicate those rare moments of insight to all hours of our life." Likewise, we accept with gratitude Heschel's emphasis on the biblical sources of our faith.

The chief question is the first one, with regard to the basic relationship of Judaism and Christianity. Here is an issue that cannot be disposed of quickly and neatly. The centuries, indeed millennia, of estrangement have produced on both sides a deep-rooted suspicion, a rigid set of stereotypes, a reflex assumption of the superiority not only of one's own faith but also of one's own formulations. Christianity could hardly regard itself as a mere "extension" of Judaism, to pick up one of Heschel's words. Nor would even "culmination" be adequate. The transformation that took place under the impact of the eschatological fulfillment, in the conviction of which Christianity originated, was too radical for that. Yet the Christian's first and perhaps strongest impression upon reading Heschel is surely that of *how much we have in common.* This is true both historically and contemporaneously. It is astonishing to note how similar have been the careers of Christianity and Judaism since they separated. Both saw the creation of philosophical-theological systems in the medieval period,

Judaism pre-eminently in Maimonides and Christianity in Thomas Aquinas. Both experienced at about the same time the emergence of a Pietism in protest against an Orthodoxy. Both produced a social gospel or religious socialism in response to the travails of industrialism in the nineteenth century.

The commonality is also clearly evident in the orientation of the two faiths today and in the tasks they face, as has been seen in our review of Heschel. He is our partner in the proclamation of the Living God over against a self-confident secularism. His exposition of the reality and necessity of prayer reminds us of long-lost dimensions of Christian life. Heschel and his fellow Jews will join us in the effort to renew religious institutions, and to deal with the perennial tension between form and dynamics, tradition and innovation in the faith community. We stand together in the effort to discern the meaning of man's true humanity, to preserve and to protect it against the "monsters of absurdity" that are rampant in our time.

Between Christianity and Judaism, however, there is not only convergence but divergence; if this were not so, they would not remain separate faith communities. The second great impression that the Christian gains from a study of Heschel's works, beyond that of what we have in common, is—not so much that there are differences (this is to be taken for granted), but that of *how much these differences are worth discussing.* They are worth discussing precisely because they are "divergences" from a common root, not simply stark contrasts such as might be found between religions of quite different origins, e.g., Christianity and Buddhism. It is questionable whether Christianity and Judaism ought to be spoken of as two different "religions," in the plural. The relationship is too intimate for that. Recall the catalogue offered by the apostle Paul of what God has granted to the Jews, in the same passage in his Letter to the Romans where he makes the poignant statement (vs. 3): "For I could wish that I myself were accursed and cut off from Christ for the sake of my brethren, my kinsmen by race."

> They are Israelites, and to them belong the sonship, the glory, the covenants, the giving of the law, the worship, and the promises; to them belong the patriarchs, and of their race, according to the flesh, is the Christ. God who is over all be blessed for ever. Amen.
>
> (Romans 9:4-5)

It is precisely this common rootedness (an image used by Paul himself in his analogy of the olive tree into which the Gentiles were being grafted) that makes it worth tracing out very carefully just where, and why, the divergences occur.

Consider for example the question of faith and works, which is central both in Christianity's critique of Judaism and—as may be seen in Heschel—in Judaism's critique of Christianity. "God asks for the heart," Heschel quotes from the Talmud. Yes, he adds, but does God ask for the heart alone? Are not deeds required as well? His answer, as we know, is a "both-and." Both *kavanah,* right intention, and the actual performance of the *mitzvah* are required. Therefore neither the Pauline principle of justification by faith without the works of the law, nor its Lutheran restatement, nor the similar views of Ritschl, Barth, and Kierkegaard are acceptable. Heschel passes all of these in review within the space of three short paragraphs![16] Nor, he adds, is the philosophical transcription of this doctrine in the form of the Kantian dictum that "there is nothing good but a good will" any more adequate. But by thus equating the Pauline and Lutheran view with the Kantian dispositional ethic, Heschel shows that he has not fully grasped the former. By "faith" in the phrase "justification by faith" is not meant some particular quality or attitude of man by virtue of which he gains God's favor, nor does the category pertain, in the first instance, to the realm of morality as such. It refers, rather, to man's whole standing before the Creator, to his being rather than his doing, to the center of his selfhood rather than its expressions. At this level, the stance implied in the notion of justification by faith is not at all dissimilar, it seems to me, to that inculcated by Heschel himself when he stresses God's initiative and man's receptivity, the attitudes of awe and appreciation (perhaps equivalents to Luther's "fear and love" of God), and the fact that man's selfhood is not self-posited but grounded in the thought and will of Another.

Christians, on their part, have worked with stereotypes of Judaism as being legalistic and moralistic, stressing God's judgment to the exclusion of his mercy, etc., certainly none of which are true of Heschel's views. Heschel can sum up his whole "doctrine of God" in the following affirmation: "Beyond the mind is mystery, but behind the mystery is mercy."[17] And compassion is one of the keynotes in his interpretation of the divine pathos. It has been forgotten, too, that Paul in enunciating his famous principle was actually quoting from the Old Testament: *"As it is written,* 'The just shall live by faith' " (Romans 1:17, referring to Habakkuk 2:4).[18] Further, it is "our forefather Abraham" whom Paul cites as the prime example of one who was justified by faith rather than works (Romans 4).

The problem of faith and works, Christianity should frankly admit, is a problem within its own thought as well as between it and Judaism. Roman Catholicism and Lutheranism came to blows upon this issue, as did Lutheranism and Calvinism (the question of the "uses of the law" and the relation between faith and obedience). We still have not reckoned fully with the motif of reward in the teaching of Jesus, nor with such Pauline assertions as that "he will render to every man according to his works" (Romans 2:6) or that "it is not the hearers of the law who are righteous before God, but the doers of the law who will be justified" (2:13). And in recent years, critics from within the Christian camp have rightly noted that an exaggeration or misinterpretation of the principle of justification by faith has often led to the preaching of a "cheap grace" which has vitiated the ethical rigor of the Christian life and, in not a few instances, has undercut the sense of historical responsibility.

The point is that the issue is sufficiently complex, and closely enough related to problems of interpretation in both Old and New Testaments, that Christians can well consider a Jewish theologian such as Abraham Heschel a partner in the process of reconsidering what they do mean or ought to mean by this cardinal doctrine, and of re-envisioning its relevance to contemporary life. We all agree on two basic tenets: *God is gracious* and *man is responsible*. The problem is how to relate the two.

This is but an example of issues that might be on the agenda for discussion between Jews and Christians. We have only opened up the problem here. A thorough discussion would require a retracing of the whole course of Paul's dialectic in the epistles to the Romans and Galatians, not to speak of subsequent controversies. What can be said is that the discussion will have far greater richness and realism if carried out in dialogue with Jewish thought than if Christians go it alone. The same is true of the Christian approach to the whole New Testament. It is amazing how the teachings of Jesus gain in depth and clarity when read against the background of Jewish thought and life, not only prior to and contemporaneous with his own career, but also subsequently—for the tradition is tenacious, and later expressions of it can illumine the earlier. Especially important is the realization of the *diversity* of the Jewish tradition, a point which we have learned to appreciate from our study of the various facets of it reflected in Heschel himself. This makes it comprehensible that such different types of literature—including the Gospel of John, once thought to be more Hellenistic than Hebraic—could arise out of the Jewish milieu of New Testament times. It helps us to understand, too, how the seemingly anti-Jewish material in the New Testament (denunciations of the scribes and Pharisees, priests and elders, and even "the Jews" collectively) can be viewed as part of the continual rivalry among Jewish factions and the work of Judaism's internal critics and reformers. As scholars have noted, on the basis of such materials as the Dead Sea Scrolls, "A great deal of the anti-Semitic imagery of the New Testament is actually a reflection of sectarian Jewish thought and rhetoric."[19]

But are there limits to interfaith dialogue? Are there topics that are taboo? Professor Heschel, in a memorable address delivered to the convention of the interfaith Religious Education Association in Chicago in the autumn of 1966, on the subject "What We Might Do Together," reviewed the common challenge presented to the several faiths by the social and cultural crisis in America today, and their common calling "to inspire the world with the biblical image of man." So far as explicitly theological discussion is concerned, however, he suggested that there ought to be some rules for interreligious dialogue. "An example of such a rule for Catholics and Protestants would be not to discuss the supremacy of the bishop of Rome or Papacy; an example of such a rule for Christians and Jews would be not to discuss Christology."[20]

With these strictures, we must respectfully disagree. The Catholic-Protestant dialogue has been able to bear the opening up of the delicate question referred to. I believe that the Jewish-Christian dialogue would prove equally resilient. However—and this is a very important "however"—the hesitance of Heschel is fully understandable in the light of the way in which the name of Christ has been used so frequently in past centuries to bludgeon the Jews, to force them to be baptized under the threat of loss of citizenship, of all human rights, and even the threat of death. The question of Christology is certainly not the question with which to begin the dialogue. It can be broached only after a long process of rebuilding openness and trust.

To say this is not to reintroduce the notion of "mission"

under the guise of "dialogue," as many Jews, including Abraham Heschel, would suspect. The point is that Christology—in the sense of Messiahship—is a question in and for Judaism itself. It is a Jewish question. Jews, therefore, can help us to frame the question properly, and thus to discern more accurately the meaning of the answer which Christians believe Jesus of Nazareth embodies.

For a long time it was customary to contrast Christianity and Judaism in this way: Christianity believes that the Messianic Age has already come, that fulfillment is to be found in a past event of history and in the influence that streams from that event. Judaism, in contrast, still looks for such fulfillment in the future. Fundamentally, that contrast is still correct; but not in quite so simple a manner as was thought. The recent "theology of hope" has reminded us that if the Messianic hope is interpreted, as it should be, in terms of its prophetic and apocalyptic background—namely, as involving the hope for a transformation of the entire cosmos, including the socio-political dimension—then it will be seen that the Christian faith also still involves an element of expectation. These theologians, indeed, would assert that such expectation provides not merely an element but the fundamental theme of the Christian proclamation. Conversely, we have seen in our study of Heschel that Judaism, for its part, does involve a strong element of present realization—whether expressed in terms of mystic immediacy, of Sabbath piety, or of the encountering of God's presence, the *Shechinah,* among the commonplaces of everyday life. Christianity is still relatively more sacramental (present-oriented) and Judaism more prophetic (future-oriented), but the problem of "the now and the not yet" is a problem for them both.

The word "dialogue" has been much overused in recent years. It can imply something only momentary or superficial. Yet is it basically a good term for the relationship which one would wish to see between Judaism and Christianity, for it has several constructive connotations. The first is that it is the task of both parties at times to speak and at times to listen. There is something to teach and something to learn; there are questions to ask and questions to answer. It implies, too, a fully human meeting, for it is not only minds that "dialogue," but total persons, total traditions, total life-styles. And the term is useful because it implies the necessity of taking seriously what is on the other fellow's mind, not only one's own. For Christians, this means at the present time, for example, taking seriously the profound concern of Jews everywhere for the fate of the State of Israel, which has completed barely two decades of precarious existence. For Jews, its means taking seriously the Christian's irrepressible urge to talk about the most central tenets of his faith, even at the cost of being thought to be cheaply proselytizing.

We have examined the promise of Abraham Joshua Heschel—for Judaism itself, for Christianity, and for all who are concerned with the humanity of man. Frequently we have let him speak for himself, for in the case of this eminently poetic theologian, the manner of what he says is often as important as the matter. Like Kierkegaard's, his writings are intended to edify, not merely to inform. We have put some questions to him, and he, in prophetic fashion, has also left us with some disturbing questions. That, too, is part of the promise of his theology.

Notes

For publication data on the books and articles by Heschel cited below, see Bibliography.

Chapter I.   A Prophetic Voice in Our Midst

1. *The Prophets,* p. 5.
2. *The Insecurity of Freedom,* pp. 87-88, 93, 96.
3. *Vietnam: Crisis of Conscience,* p. 49.
4. *The Insecurity of Freedom,* p. 39.
5. *Ibid.,* pp. 70ff.
6. This latter half was omitted in the paperback edition of *The Prophets* published in 1969.
7. "No Religion Is an Island," p. 117.
8. On the Soviet question, see *The Insecurity of Freedom,* chapters 18 and 19. On the State of Israel, see Heschel's book *Israel: An Echo of Eternity.*
9. Cf. *Israel,* p. 112.
10. *Who Is Man?* p. 105.

Chapter II.   God as Presence and Pathos

1. "No Religion Is an Island," p. 117.
2. *Funk and Wagnalls Standard College Dictionary* (New York, 1968).
3. *Man Is Not Alone,* pp. 5-6.
4. "The Mystical Element in Judaism," p. 602. This essay by Heschel is an invaluable survey of the subject. For a more extended treatment see Gershom G. Scholem, *Major Trends in Jewish Mysticism* (New York: Schocken Books, 1946).
5. Martin Buber published many works on the Hasidic movement. For a sociological study of the Brooklyn community, see Solomon Poll, *The Hasidic Community of Williamsburg: A*

Study in the Sociology of Religion (New York: Schocken Books, 1969). The word is also sometimes spelled "Chassidic."

6. *Man Is Not Alone*, p. 55.

7. "The Mystical Element in Judaism," p. 603.

8. *Man Is Not Alone*, p. 78; *Who Is Man?* p. 92.

9. *God in Search of Man*, p. 147.

10. *The Insecurity of Freedom*, pp. 289-290.

11. The following is a paraphrase of Heschel's discussion in *The Prophets*, pp. 221ff.

12. *The Prophets*, p. 48.

13. Dietrich Bonhoeffer, *Letters and Papers from Prison* (3rd ed.; New York: Macmillan, 1967), p. 197.

14. *The Prophets*, pp. 271-272.

15. *Ibid.*, p. 487. On the theme of God as "place," see *Man Is Not Alone*, p. 150, and *The Sabbath*, pp. 114-115 (from the appended essay on "Space, Time, and Reality"). On the question of God as "person," cf. *The Prophets*, pp. 273, 486.

Chapter III.   The Meaning of Being Human

1. See Meland's *Faith and Culture* (New York: Oxford, 1953) and other works.

2. *Man Is Not Alone*, p. 45.

3. *Ibid.*, p. 133.

4. *Ibid.*, pp. 128-129.

5. *Ibid.*, p. 129.

6. *Ibid.*, pp. 194-195.

7. *Ibid.*, chaps. 4 and 19.

8. *Ibid.*, p. 203.

9. As rendered by Heschel in *The Prophets*, p. 13.

10. *The Prophets*, p. 4.

11. From the essay as printed in *Man's Quest for God*, pp. 147-151.

12. *The Insecurity of Freedom*, p. 165 (from Heschel's address entitled "Sacred Image of Man").

13. *Israel*, p. 94.

14. *Ibid.*, p. 97.

15. *Ibid.*, p. 127.

16. *Ibid.*, p. 128.

17. *Ibid.*, p. 132.

18. *Ibid.*, pp. 220-221, 223.

19. *God in Search of Man*, p. 377.

20. *Israel,* p. 159.

21. *Man Is Not Alone*, p. 243.

22. *The Prophets*, p. 484. Cf. *God in Search of Man*, pp. 127-128.

23. Brief citations in the following paragraphs are all from *Who Is Man?*

24. *Who Is Man?* p. 119.

25. *The Insecurity of Freedom*, pp. 152-153 (from the essay "Sacred Image of Man").

Chapter IV.   Religious Tradition and Contemporary Life-Style

1. *The Insecurity of Freedom*, pp. 204ff.

2. *Man Is Not Alone*, p. 173.

3. *God in Search of Man*, p. 3.

4. *Israel*, p. 224.

5. *Funk and Wagnalls Standard College Dictionary* (New York, 1968).

6. *Who Is Man?* pp. 98-99.

7. *The Earth Is the Lord's,* pp. 8-10. The following paragraphs will contain many brief allusions to this book; only longer quotations will be specifically identified by page.

8. *Ibid.*, p. 76.

9. *Ibid.*, p. 16.

10. *Ibid.*, pp. 18-20.

11. *Ibid.*, p. 34.

12. *Ibid.*, pp. 30-31.

13. *The Sabbath,* pp. 3ff. For earlier developments of this theme see *The Earth Is the Lord's*, p. 7; *Man Is Not Alone*, p. 200; *God in Search of Man*, p. 206.

14. *The Sabbath*, p. 100.

15. *Ibid.*, p. 8.

16. E.g., John Marsh in his article in *A Theological Word Book of the Bible,* ed. Alan Richardson (New York: Macmillan, 1951), which despite later controversy remains a valuable resource.

17. *Man Is Not Alone*, p. 205.

18. *The Insecurity of Freedom*, pp. 70-84.

19. *The Sabbath*, p. 27; *Israel*, p. 160.

20. *The Sabbath,* p. 28.

Chapter V.   Worship, Learning, Action

1. *God in Search of Man*, p. 31. This provides the organizing principle for the three sections of this book.

2. As rendered in modern translation by the novelist Herman Wouk in his testament of Jewish faith, *This Is My God* (New York: Doubleday, 1961), pp. 303ff.

3. "The Mystical Element in Judaism," pp. 603-604.

4. *The Prophets*, p. 483.

5. *Man's Quest for God*, pp. 5ff.

6. *God in Search of Man*, p. 49.

7. *Man's Quest for God*, p. 62.

8. *The Insecurity of Freedom*, p. 255, in Heschel's lecture given at Union Theological Seminary on "Prayer as Discipline."

9. *Ibid.* On the rejection of the personal analogy, see also *Man's Quest for God*, p. 10.

10. *Man's Quest for God*, p. 95.

11. *God in Search of Man*, p. 129.

12. *Ibid.*, p. 239.

13. *Ibid.*, p. 274.

14. *Ibid.*, p. 255.

15. *Man Is Not Alone,* p. 168.

16. *The Insecurity of Freedom*, p. 119; and see the whole essay on "Depth Theology," pp. 115-126. Cf. also *God in Search of Man*, pp. 6ff.

17. *God in Search of Man*, p. 283. Cf. above, p. 57.

18. *Ibid.*, pp. 338, 339.

19. *The Insecurity of Freedom*, p. 44.

20. *Who Is Man?* p. 100.

21. *Man Is Not Alone*, p. 263.

22. *God in Search of Man*, p. 399.

23. *God in Search of Man*, p. 366.

24. *Ibid.*, pp. 378-379.

25. *Reinhold Niebuhr: His Religious, Social, and Political Thought*, ed. by Charles W. Kegley and Robert W. Bretall (New York: Macmillan, 1956). Heschel's chapter, originally entitled "A Hebrew Evaluation of Reinhold Niebuhr," was republished in *The Insecurity of Freedom* under the title "Confusion of Good and Evil" (pp. 127-149).

26. *The Insecurity of Freedom*, p. 127.

27. *Ibid.*, p. 139.

28. *Ibid.*, pp. 144-145. Cf. *God in Search of Man,* p. 378.

29. *The Insecurity of Freedom,* pp. 143-144.

Chapter VI.   Encounter between Christianity and Judaism

1. *The Insecurity of Freedom*, p. 187.

2. For an interpretation of anti-Semitism as symptomatic of a malady in Western culture as a whole, see Aarne Siirala, *The Voice of Illness: A Study in Therapy and Prophecy* (Philadelphia: Fortress, 1964).

3. *The Insecurity of Freedom*, p. 93.

4. *Cross Currents*, Vol. II, No. 2 (Spring, 1952), pp. 35-42.

5. *Ibid.*, p. 42.

6. "No Religion Is an Island," p. 125.

7. Rabbi Samuel Dresner, in *Proceedings of the Rabbinical Assembly: Sixty-Eighth Annual Convention* (New York: The Rabbinical Assembly, 1968), p. 187.

8. See Will Herberg, review of Heschel's *God in Search of Man*, in *Christian Century*, Vol. LXXIII, No. 16 (April 18, 1956), p. 486; Emil Fackenheim, "God in Search of Man," *Conservative Judaism*, Vol. XV, No. 1 (Fall, 1960), pp. 50-53; Maurice Friedman, "Abraham Joshua Heschel: The Philosopher of Wonder," *Congress Bi-Weekly*, Vol. 34, No. 17 (December 18, 1967), pp. 12-14; Jakob Petuchowski, "Faith as the Leap of Action: The Theology of Abraham Joshua Heschel," *Commentary*, Vol. XXVII, No. 1 (January, 1959), pp. 23-29; Jacob Neusner, review of Heschel's *Torah min ha-shamayim,* in *Conservative Judaism,* Vol. XX, No. 3 (Spring, 1966), pp. 66-73. Details on the Cohen and Borowitz volumes are given in the Bibliography below.

9. The liberal criticisms are summarized in Cohen's *The Natural and the Supernatural Jew*. For an orthodox critique, dwelling chiefly on Heschel's concept of "anthropopathism," see Eliezer Berkovits, "Dr. A. J. Heschel's Theology of Pathos," *Tradition: A Journal of Orthodox Thought*, Vol. VI, No. 2 (Spring-Summer, 1964), pp. 67-104.

10. From Niebuhr's review of *Man Is Not Alone*, in *New York Herald-Tribune Book Review*, April 1, 1951.

11. *The Insecurity of Freedom*, p. 217 (from the essay "Israel and Diaspora"). For other aspects of Heschel's critique of

Judaism, see the whole last section of this volume.

12. *Ibid.*, pp. 3-4. From Heschel's address at the seminar on Religion in a Free Society sponsored by the Fund for the Republic, May 9, 1958. First printed as "The Religious Message," in John Cogley, ed., *Religion in America* (New York: Meridian, 1958).

13. See *Christian Century*, Vol. LXXX, No. 49 (December 4, 1963), pp. 1501-1504, or the text of the article as reprinted in *The Insecurity of Freedom*, pp. 168-178.

14. *The Insecurity of Freedom*, pp. 169-170.

15. *Ibid.*, p. 175.

16. *God in Search of Man*, pp. 293-294.

17. *Ibid.*, p. 353.

18. AV; RSV: "He who through faith is righteous shall live." The different nuances in the Old and New Testament texts are accounted for in part at least by the fact that Paul was quoting from the Greek translation, the Septuagint.

19. Jacob B. Agus, in *Bulletin, Lutheran Theological Seminary, Gettysburg, Pennsylvania*, Vol. 48, No. 2 (Spring, 1968), p. 42.

20. "What We Might Do Together," p. 140.

21. "The Mystical Element in Judaism," p. 607.

Bibliography

Works by Abraham J. Heschel

Books

The Earth Is the Lord's: The Inner Life of the Jew in East Europe. New York: Henry Schuman, 1950.

The Sabbath: Its Meaning for Modern Man. New York: Farrar, Straus, and Young, 1951. Expanded edition, reprinted in one volume with *The Earth Is the Lord's*, New York: Meridian, 1963. Citations for both books are to the expanded, one-volume edition.

Man Is Not Alone: A Philosophy of Religion. New York: Farrar, Straus, and Young, 1951.

Man's Quest for God: Studies in Prayer and Symbolism. New York: Scribner's, 1954.

God in Search of Man: A Philosophy of Judaism. New York: Farrar, Straus, and Cudahy, 1955.

The Prophets. New York: Harper, 1962.

The Insecurity of Freedom: Essays on Human Existence. New York: Farrar, Straus, and Giroux, 1965.

Who Is Man? Stanford, Calif.: Stanford University Press, 1965.

Israel: An Echo of Eternity. New York: Farrar, Straus, and Giroux, 1969.

Maimonides: Eine Biographie. Berlin: Erich Reiss, 1935.

Die Prophetie. Cracow: Polish Academy of Sciences, 1936.

Torah min ha-shamayim be-ispaklaryah shel ha-dorot (Hebrew) London and New York: Soncino Press, Vol. I, 1962; Vol. II, 1965.

Essays and Articles (selected)

"The Mystical Element in Judaism," in Louis Finkelstein (ed.), *The Jews: Their History, Culture, and Religion*. 4 vols. New York: Harper, 1949. Pp. 602-623.

"No Religion Is an Island," in *Union Seminary Quarterly Review*, Vol. XXI, No. 2, Part I (January, 1966), pp. 117-134.

"What We Might Do Together," in *Religious Education*, Vol. LXII, No. 2 (March-April, 1967), pp. 133-140.

"The Jewish Notion of God and Christian Renewal," in *Renewal of Religious Thought: Proceedings of the Congress on the Theology of the Renewal of the Church, Centenary of Canada, 1867-1967*. Dorval, Quebec: Palm Publishers, n.d.

For a complete bibliography of Heschel's writings to 1965, including some seventy-five articles, essays, and reviews, see Fritz A. Rothschild (ed.), *Between God and Man: An Interpretation of Judaism, From the Writings of Abraham J. Heschel* (New York: Free Press, 1959).

Discussions of Heschel's Thought (selected)

Bird, Thomas E. (ed.). *Modern Theologians: Christians and Jews*. Notre Dame, Ind.: University of Notre Dame Press, and New York: Association Press, 1967. Pp. 169-182.

Borowitz, Eugene B. *A New Jewish Theology in the Making*. Philadelphia: Westminster, 1968. Chap. VII.

Cherbonnier, Edmond LaB. "Heschel as a Religious Thinker." *Conservative Judaism*, Vol. XXIII, No. 1 (Fall, 1968), pp 25-39.

Cohen, Arthur A., *The Natural and the Supernatural Jew: An Historical and Theological Introduction*. New York: Pantheon, 1962. Chap. III.

Granfield, Patrick, *Theologians at Work*. New York: Macmillan, 1967. Pp. 69-85.

Rothschild, Fritz A. "Introduction" to *Between Man and Man* (see above).

———,"The Religious Thought of Abraham Heschel." *Conservative Judaism*, Vol. XXIII (Fall, 1968), pp. 12-24.

Sherman, Franklin, "Abraham Joshua Heschel: Spokesman for Jewish Faith." *Lutheran World*, Vol. X, No. 4 (October, 1963), pp. 400-408.

See also the book reviews and articles mentioned in notes 8 and 9 of Chap. VI.